THE DON'T SWEAT GUIDE
TO ENTERTAINING

Other books by the editors of Don't Sweat Press

THE DON'T SWEAT GUIDE TO ENTERTAINING

Enjoying Friends More While Worrying Less

By the Editors of Don't Sweat Press
Foreword by Richard Carlson, Ph.D.

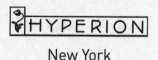

New York

Contents

Foreword

I just threw a big party for Kris's birthday, so entertaining is fresh in my mind. Therefore, it's not only a great time for me to write this foreword, it's an honor, as well!

While I've always acknowledged that entertaining can certainly be stressful at times, I do believe that, given the right attitude, much of that stress can be set aside. In other words, as hard as it is to admit, at least some of that stress is self-imposed. That's why I believe that this book can be so helpful.

The editors of Don't Sweat Press have done an outstanding job of reminding all of us that while entertaining is indeed a lot of work, most of the time, it's also supposed to be fun! Whether we're entertaining friends, family, or business associates, it's a joy to make others smile and have a good time. It doesn't have to be a serious occasion that makes you tense and uptight.

The strategies in this book have been designed to take much of the stress out of entertaining. They have been written in a way that gets us to think a little bit outside the box so we can be creative, have a good time, delegate some of the work, and minimize the hassles, while maximizing the fun! We can cut costs, save time, and enhance enjoyment, all at once!

So often, when we throw a party or plan an event, we become obsessed with every last detail, but in our obsession to get everything just right, the stress that we create interferes with our own effectiveness. We end up stumbling around, making mistakes, getting uptight, and most importantly, not having any fun at our own functions. We can even make people mad in the process, including some of the people who are helping us—or even those that we have hired to work for us. The most striking examples of this phenomenon are seen at weddings (see *The Don't Sweat Guide for Weddings*), where it's sometimes the case that brides and grooms are the only ones not having any fun! How very sad, indeed.

I believe that this book is a must-read for anyone who is planning to throw a party or do any type of entertaining, anytime soon. Any single idea can potentially make the difference between having a negative experience and a positive one. So often, the slightest shift has an enormous impact. I hope that this book helps you as much as it has me, and that, most importantly, the next time you throw a party, you have a wonderful time!

Richard Carlson
Benicia, California, 2004

THE DON'T SWEAT GUIDE
TO ENTERTAINING

1.

Know Why You're Doing It

Entertaining has the potential to fill you with creativity, dread, energy, fear, joy, or some simmering stew of emotions that you may not even be able to identify. Your response to the demands of entertaining may vary from one event to another, depending on the guests, the occasion, and what's going on in the rest of your life. You can keep the stress level down by taking the time to understand what you're doing and why.

Are your plans business-related—schmoozing with colleagues or impressing the boss? Is it your turn to host a traditional family gathering? Have you invited some of your favorite people, just for the sheer pleasure of their company? Do you simply feel an obligation to return the hospitality of others? Each of these circumstances calls for a mindset of its own and has its own desired results. If you're at all vague about why you're hosting an event, take a moment to sort out your reasons.

Understand that you are making a choice when you entertain. You could have chosen otherwise, but you didn't. This reality needs

15

to be at the forefront of your mind, especially in the case of "obligatory" entertaining. It's all too easy to resent responsibilities that you feel you must assume, regardless of your intrinsic interest in or enjoyment of them. When you accept that you made the choice to do this and that you have good reasons for what you are doing, you can shed the self-pity and get on with doing a good job that will give you satisfaction and joy.

Understand your aim, as well. You may want to express your love and appreciation, make yourself a recognizable face in an otherwise anonymous business culture, or just have a blast. Whatever your aim, you need to let it dictate all of the decisions that you make if you want to entertain successfully.

Keep your reason for entertaining in focus throughout the process. Whether you're throwing a no-fuss picnic or staging an elaborate, formal celebration, every act of hospitality can lead to moments of weariness, rush, or uncertainty. When the less pleasurable moments of planning and executing arise, let your essential motivation—the "why" that got you into it in the first place—be the fuel that keeps you going.

2.

What's Your Style?

Although some folks still choose to follow old patterns and "rules" for entertaining and hosting events, in reality, we live in a time that tolerates—even invites—a lot of individuality. People think less about what they're "supposed" to do, and more about the charm and interest of making an event what they want it to be. You are largely free to do your entertaining in whatever way suits you best.

So what *does* suit you best? Do you have a great fondness for a lovely setting, or do you prefer the picnic feel of paper plates and bright colors? Are you an amateur gourmet chef, or does the ease of a potluck gathering give you a lift? Do you like to host a cocktail hour with a few fancy finger foods, a weekend brunch without the multiple courses of a more formal meal, or a game night that features activity instead of food and drink?

If you feel most comfortable with an informal social scene, you may find a complicated or elaborate event more than you care to plan or carry out. That's okay. Even weddings and other traditionally fancy events can be full of warmth, charm, and good times without getting into a lot of expense. You can choose a theme that emphasizes the flavor of fun that you want, and carry it out on a modest scale and a moderate budget.

If you are uninspired by the ultra-simple, you can turn even the most casual entertaining into an event to remember by adding unique touches. Handmade name cards, unusual napkin holders, lavish fresh flowers, an ethnic theme that adds color and texture—the possibilities are endless.

The point is simply this: You will feel the least amount of stress and the greatest satisfaction when you entertain in a way that matches your personal style. Aiming for some goal that isn't "you" is usually a recipe for anxiety. Making the most of who you are and what pleases you will allow you to relax and enjoy the process, as well as the product.

3.

Consider Your Guests

Generally speaking, you will have some prior knowledge of the people that you entertain. You'll know their personal styles, whether conservative or flamboyant, quiet or outgoing. You may know, as well, the sorts of foods or activities that they prefer, their favorite drinks, and the company that they seem to enjoy. All of this offers you a head start as you plan your entertaining. While it makes sense to suit your own styles and tastes when you play host, it will only lead to frustration and disappointment if you hold fast to choices that you know might make your guests uncomfortable.

Consider who your guests are and what they like. If you know them well, focus on ways that you can suit every one of them in at least some token way. Keep them in mind as you choose the music that you play in the background, the way that you light the space, and whether you sit outside or inside. If you are serving food, use the "on the side" option with any dish that includes extras such as nuts, dressings, sauces, or additional butter, so that people can eliminate or cut back on items that may not suit them. Let people serve themselves so that they can limit amounts or sidestep dislikes as desired. If you are serving alcoholic beverages, make sure that you provide nonalcoholic beverages as an alternative for nondrinkers. If you plan to play games, be prepared with optional ways that an individual can be involved in the event that he or she does not want to play.

You may be entertaining people that you do not know—at least not well. In that case, it's always a good idea to do some gentle probing ahead of time. Make sure that you let people know if you have a lot of steps to climb or particularly steep stairs. Check ahead for any food allergies, dairy intolerance, or salt limitations. Consider, if relevant, the possibility of food restrictions having to do with religious or ethnic beliefs. Never be afraid to ask ahead of time: "Is there anything that you don't eat?" or "Are there any party games that you might not enjoy playing?" You will communicate to your guests that they are important and that you are happy to make their needs a part of your preparation.

4.

Be Yourself

There's no question that you have a unique role to play when entertaining others. You're the one who orchestrates the action. You make sure that your guests feel welcome and comfortable, that they are provided with what they need, and that they are having a good time. For the duration of your entertaining, you don the host hat and take responsibility for the party's success. Playing the host role does not mean, however, that you have to turn into someone other than yourself. Part of what sets guests at ease and heightens their enjoyment is the knowledge that you are having a good time.

Being yourself in the midst of entertaining can be harder than it sounds. The details and work involved can sometimes make it difficult to relax into a natural, appealing version of yourself. You may find yourself distracted, anxious, edgy, or rushed, which in turn may make it difficult to join in the good experience that you want to offer your guests. If you think back over past experiences, you can probably see how the stresses of entertaining got in your way. Simply recognizing this can be the first important step toward a more natural and enjoyable experience of hosting in the future.

Let the past be your teacher. In a quiet moment—not when company is walking up your front path—review your past experiences. Take the time to isolate the specifics that caused you stress. Perhaps your issues had to do with time or money; maybe you were uptight because you needed more help or fewer guests; or maybe it was a matter of too elaborate a plan. Whatever the source of stress, it robbed you of the best experience that you could have had and deprived your guests of the "you" that they said "yes" to in the first place.

Once you've identified the particular issues that tend to stress you out when you host a gathering, you can begin to strategize to offset those issues. Experiment by making a change in just one of the areas that causes you stress, and see how it helps. Then tackle another item on the stress list. Over time, such an approach can become a habit that keeps you relaxed and happy during your entertaining.

Much of what makes you who you are is hardwired into your makeup. It may be obscured behind the effects of anxiety or weariness, but it's still there. The key to being yourself in the midst of entertaining is to rid yourself of the stress-produced camouflage, and the key to *that* is changing what you do and how you think—not who you are.

5.

Establish Priorities

When it comes to managing or eliminating stress—whether it's associated with entertaining or any other facet of life—nothing helps more than the ability to discern what is important and what is not. You may have a list of twenty-five concerns as you plan or carry out an event, but you can be sure that they are not all crucial to the success of your event.

When you're planning to entertain, go ahead and make your list. Then consider which of the items on the list could be simplified or eliminated if need be. Identify *when* items need to be accomplished. Put a big star next to the ones that are so important that if you don't get to them, you put the success of your event at risk.

Prioritizing is an invaluable skill to develop for every area of life. The establishing of priorities allows you to intelligently use your resources—time, money, physical energy, or attention. Even better, it helps you maintain a realistic sense of what's important, so that when the inevitable entertaining glitches occur, you can carry on with a minimum of fuss.

6.

Be Realistic

When we plan to entertain, we daydream about new combinations of guests, venues, themes, and activities. However, take care when you rev up the dream machine. It's fun to think big, but if you want to keep stress to a minimum, you need to plant your feet on solid ground in regard to what you can actually manage.

When you get ready to entertain, take a realistic look at your life. Check your time commitments, and gauge exactly how much time you have available, not only for the event itself, but for the shopping, cleaning, preparation, and whatever else will be involved. Finding that you have little time should not prevent you from inviting people over, but you may want to adjust what you do and on what scale. You can satisfy the entertaining bug with a simple evening of pizza and a video and save the full, four-course dinner for twelve for some time when you have a break from other commitments.

Consider the expense of your dream event, as well. Be realistic about what you can afford. Committing yourself to credit card debt for the sake of a big bash is a sure recipe for stress. Assess what portion of your discretionary funds you want to apply to a one-time event. Will you regret spending money on an extravaganza when it's time to replace the roof or send your child to camp? Again, taking a realistic approach to how much you'll spend on entertaining doesn't mean that you have to shelve the idea altogether. You simply need to adjust your vision until it lines up with what you'd actually like to spend.

Finally, take a hard look at whether you'll enjoy all that your dream party would entail. Granted, the perfect setting with all of the trimmings has its appeal, but are you really up for hand-lettering the name cards, preparing individual favors, polishing the heirloom silver, butterflying a dozen Cornish hens for the grill, and stringing up a mile of twinkle lights?

Dreaming brings out the kid in us. Acting on our dreams without regular reality checks brings adult problems crashing down on our heads. Get real from the start, and let your dreams do their part without getting you in a jam.

7.

Choose Your Moments

While some entertaining has more to do with social obligation than fun and games, all of it can include friendly conversation, pleasure, respite from work, and a change of pace. However, it delivers its greatest benefits when you choose your moments thoughtfully.

Rather than let entertaining back you into a corner, take a proactive approach. When the holidays hit and parties and family gatherings are a dime a dozen, consider an alternative timeframe for your contribution. Plan ahead into the after-holiday doldrums, and get your *future* gig on the calendar, rather than staging one more (unneeded) event in the midst of the frenzy.

Instead of focusing on the tried and true Friday or Saturday get-togethers of modern life, think about whether a midweek event might provide more of a break—especially if you plan an evening that you can prepare ahead (over the previous weekend, for example, when you don't have professional obligations). You can also look for the spontaneous midweek possibilities. Invite a few friends in for pizza and a public TV special on television. Throw together an impromptu sunset event on an unusually lovely autumn evening, with simple cocktail fare as your offering.

To spread out the fun over times and seasons that are typically less crowded with socializing, take advantage of the benchmarks and little victories of life. Hold mini-celebrations that add festivity to everyday accomplishments by recognizing and honoring them. A project that turned out well, a change of job, a course of study completed, or an unconventional anniversary ("It's three years since I got out of the leg cast!") can offer a pretext for timing your entertaining to fit your overall schedule.

Don't let the conventions of entertaining press you into high-stress mode. Take charge by making the most of the quieter times. You'll offer fun to others when it will be most appreciated, and you'll give yourself the leisure to enjoy what you're doing.

8.

Find a Focus

It's easy to get carried away if you're an enthusiast about food and entertaining. With company coming, you pull out all the stops, gather gourmet recipes for everything from soup to nuts, and build a dining event that aims to astound. Unfortunately, while you're at it, you complicate your plans to such an extent that preparation becomes onerous. Your love of great food falls prey to overload, and your guests have too much of a good thing to deal with.

Even some of the best-known chefs and finest restaurants take care not to overdo special presentations. There's an art to choosing the focus of a great dining experience, and it's one that is worth mastering.

The first step is to find the one or two elements of your event that you want to highlight. For these, you may pay more for the ingredients, spend more time in the preparation, and give more attention to how you present the dish. If you're a wine aficionado, you can make the wine courses the point of the meal, choosing simple flavors that show off the wine instead of competing with it.

Once you've chosen the star performer, you can surround it with much simpler, faster-to-prepare items. If you're serving meat or fish that is best eaten without undue additions, you may choose to create a fabulous salad, unique homemade bread, or an array of small side dishes that complement the simple main item. If the meat is an elaborate dish, you can stick to more straightforward sides that rely on color and texture instead of complexity.

The focused approach to entertaining with food allows you to control the fuss without sacrificing elegance or festivity. With less fuss over the food, you have more time, energy, and enthusiasm for your guests, who—after all—are the reason for what you're doing in the first place!

9.

Avoid Elaboration

A party can offer a wonderful opportunity to exercise your creativity, put some extra effort into decorating, and finish up that home project that you've been poking away at for months. Take care, though, that you don't let an upcoming party turn into a millstone that weighs you down with all that you have to do to be ready. It's fine to let an event provide a little extra motivation. When it becomes overbearing and stressful, you've taken on too much.

Keeping the meal simple is one way to avoid burdens. Taking care to find one element of a decorating scheme to focus on is another. A sumptuous flower arrangement does not require elaborate napkin folding, calligraphic name cards, or party favors for every guest. If you've got the time and the inclination, by all means, take it to the limit. Just remember to count the cost in time and worry ahead of time, and make sure that your preparations fit with everything else that you need to do (in your life, as well as for the party).

When you think about how you want your house, yard, garden, or patio to look for your guests, remember that most people don't see what you see. Every little chore that you haven't had time to finish, every fix-up that you haven't completed, and every failed corner of the garden may scream at you every time that you see them. Other people, less familiar with your hopes and dreams, usually won't even notice. You can guarantee that they won't pay any attention to your "problem" areas by consciously drawing attention to the things that you're happy with. Set a beautiful table, create attention-getting seating arrangements, or put out a beautiful display of appetizers, and your guests will never notice that the fence didn't get painted.

Let your entertaining plans be as simple as they need to be. Don't worry your way into making the event more complicated. Stick to the relevant details. If you have time and energy to do a little extra, great—but *treat* it as extra, a dispensable item that you'll get to if you can, but won't worry over if you can't.

10.

Honor Your Budget

Of all the stress-producers in life, an overextended financial situation has to be one of the top items on the list. With the prevalence of credit and the sophistication of the advertising industry, more people than not in modern Western society carry one degree or another of debt as a rule, rather than as an exception. This leads to an unfortunate level of ease about going into credit card debt—a much costlier type of borrowing—for expenses that would more appropriately be limited by the discretionary money that we actually have.

If you want your entertaining experience to be a good one without angst or an unpleasant aftermath, create an entertainment budget, and live within it. Make a realistic assessment of how much discretionary money you have each month. Then make a rough list of the activities and expenses that the money has to cover. Once you do that, you'll be able to gauge the maximum total amount of money that you have available for fun. You'll also have a clearer idea of the tradeoffs that might be necessary, depending on how costly you make your entertaining on a given occasion.

Whatever you do, don't fall into the trap of believing that hosting friends, family, or colleagues has to cost a bundle. Plenty of great, low-budget ideas exist for how to make your dollars stretch without the appearance of cost savings. Look in your local library for party books and cookbooks if you're having a hard time figuring out how to stage a good time at a lower cost. Make a habit of leafing through magazines that regularly feature entertainment ideas, and check out the "dining in" and "lifestyles" sections of the newspaper.

It may take a change of perspective or new habits to steer away from expensive entertaining. You may have to give it a little more planning time or exercise a bit more imagination—but the dividends in peace of mind and satisfaction will more than repay the effort, and you'll have nothing but pleasant memories to deal with when the party is over.

11.

Plan Ahead

Impromptu get-togethers and last-minute entertaining have the great advantage of low expectations on every side, but probably more often than not, you make your entertainment dates in advance. As a result, you may feel obliged to make a bigger deal of what you offer your guests than you would at the last minute. Here's the trick to meeting those expectations with the least possible stress: When you make your invitation in advance, start planning.

Advance planning means that you lay out a schedule, if only in your mind, that measures how much time you have leading up to the event, how much will need to be done for it, and what can be accomplished ahead of time. Such an approach ought to be automatic. Common sense tells you that the more you do ahead of time, the less pressure you'll feel as the time of the event nears. However, modern life tends to be full and hectic, and it often crowds out common sense. It requires an act of will and a persistent spirit to take control of your time and get things done ahead of the game.

Start deciding the details of what you'll do as soon as you have the date set and the guest list finalized. Keep a running list of what you'll have to buy and do in order to turn your plans into reality. Find the items on the list that you can take care of soonest and get going on them. Make it a goal to check off something every day.

There's more to this approach than meets the eye. It certainly cuts down on the amount of work that you'll have to do at the last minute, which in turn cuts your anxiety levels. It also gives you the time to adjust your plans without panic if some of your decisions and ideas prove impossible to implement. Perhaps your original menu calls for items that can't be found at the last minute—or you may discover that your plan calls for something that turns out to be costlier than you realized, and you need to find an alternative that fits your budget.

Any and all of these and other changes can be handled with aplomb while you still have time. If you're up against a looming calendar, they can feel like disaster and turn an otherwise happy idea into your personal nightmare. Don't let procrastination ruin your fun. Get busy the minute you know the party's on.

12.

Pace Your Preparations

There's no question that when you plan to entertain, the event itself is your focus and goal—your destination, in a sense. Most entertaining, however, requires some getting ready, and that's your journey. The more you can shape the preparation work into a process that is satisfying in its own right, the more you will transform the overall experience from work and stress into pleasure and a sense of accomplishment.

As you do your advance preparation for entertaining, it pays to reckon with what makes you happy. Different people enjoy varying ways of getting things done. Maybe you like to keep the jobs small and the time investment at any given moment short. Alternately, you may enjoy blocking out a chunk of time that you devote to making significant headway. Whatever your style, you can put it to good use as you prepare to entertain.

Make getting ready part of the fun. Do you love to crank up the stereo when you have things to do? Go for it. Put on your favorite tunes and dance your way through the cleaning. Light candles and pour yourself a glass of wine for an evening of making your hors d'oeuvres ahead of time. Make a date with a friend to get your shopping done in good company.

Be sure to avoid loading all of the hard stuff into a last-minute workday. If you've got a number of labor-intensive jobs that need to be done, spread them out over several days, if possible. Leave the easiest jobs for last so that you're not overburdened with tiring work at just the time when you need to be at your most energetic.

In the final analysis, the difference between play and work is often a matter of perspective. If you make up your mind to enjoy the journey as much as the destination, you can make the preparation for entertaining as entertaining as the final result.

13.

Face Your Limitations

Imagine a dream party. All of your favorite people have gathered in your home. You have live music on the patio; fresh flowers and glowing candles on every available surface; a smorgasbord that doesn't quit in the dining room; people in white gloves circulating with trays and drinks; a charming guest telling hilarious stories; yourself striking exactly the right tone as you move from one person to another.

Whether or not this is your idea of a dream come true, you probably have some "ideal" scenario when you think of entertaining at its best. You've seen it in the movies, read about it in a book, or watched it in some ad. There's nothing wrong with dreaming, but if you want to maximize your satisfaction and minimize your stress, clear-eyed realism will serve you a lot better.

Take an honest look at what you and your resources can handle before you get too carried away with making your entertaining dreams come true. Of course, money and time must be considered, but you also need to calculate the amount of space that you have, because it bears a direct relationship to how comfortable you can make your guests.

A large gathering at which people outnumber places to sit will limit the sort of party that you throw and how long you can expect it to last. A situation in which people need to negotiate stairs to get from one entertaining area to another will call for sensitivity in regard to people who have disabilities. It will also have a potential effect on the type of food and drink that you serve and how you serve it. A bash that depends on using outdoor space, as well as indoor space, will require extra preparation in the event of adverse conditions.

Think about your internal resources. Your temperament plays a significant role in what you can handle and what you enjoy. If large groups make you nervous or leave you cold, it makes sense to concentrate on entertaining on a smaller scale, where you, as host, can be more comfortable and relaxed. If you aren't crazy about playing host but have accumulated a large number of social obligations, you may want to plan one big gig a year as your contribution to the social scene.

It has been said that it takes a wise person to know his or her limitations. Whether you think of these in terms of personal qualities, material resources, or time commitments, you are indeed wise to know and respect your limitations when you plan to entertain. Within that knowledge lies some of your greatest strength.

14.

Be Flexible

E ven when we're in the midst of something intended to be fun, people get sick or injured, family crises arise, the dog eats the steak, or the toilet backs up. When these things befall us at exactly the moment that we were hoping for perfection, we have the choice either to bend or to hold a rigid position.

The rigid position is one in which, faced with the crisis, you have no alternative ideas. You're so thoroughly stuck on what you planned that a change is virtually unthinkable. Your imagination stalls, your composure crumbles, and you compound your discomfort by losing your temper, pouting, or sinking into a cloud of gloom.

Bending, on the other hand, presupposes the knowledge that trouble happens to everyone in life. Your flexibility grows out of self-esteem, a sense of humor, compassion for others and yourself, and perspective. You can bend, because you know that a shift in your plans is not the end of the world. It's just a passing moment that you can meet calmly with the result that you can rise to the occasion, handle the crisis, and regroup for the sake of your guests.

15.

Expect the Unpredictable

One of life's greatest joys—and challenges—is its lack of predictability. Life is organic. It plays itself out from day to day with movement and variation. Our foresight is limited and our control superficial at best.

When you entertain, you rub up against the unpredictable quality of life regularly. Not only do you deal with the usual assortment of details that can take an unexpected turn at any moment, but you willingly introduce other people into the mix, with all of their quirks in personality and temperament. You plan with a certain set of expectations in mind, but if you're wise, you'll recognize that your expectations most likely will not be fully met.

The best preparation for the unpredictable is a mindset that accepts it as reality—life as we all experience it. Knowing in advance that you can't predict the outcome of any situation makes it far easier to go with the flow when your expectations fail to match the reality. Do your best to plan, and follow through to the best of your ability. Then settle in for the ride.

Keep in mind that when the course you've set for an event doesn't go exactly as expected, you have a number of choices. In some cases, you can intervene to push things back into the mold that you intended. Alternatively, you can sit back and let the situation play itself out, with an eye to keeping your guests well cared for in the midst of it. You can also take some sort of middle course, nudging the situation along and redefining it as you go, all the time maintaining some semblance of responsibility for the ultimate success of the event.

Regardless of the choices that you make when you face the unpredictable, your ability to deal with it will be far greater when you are not surprised. It's all in the nature of life, and life is always an adventure. Be ready for it, and you'll avoid undue anxiety in the midst of it.

16.

Enjoy the Unexpected

Many of the circumstances that arise unexpectedly out of the business of entertaining can be quite delightful. A guest brings an unexpected gift. The sun breaks through at just the right moment on a day predicted to be wet and gloomy. The experimental dish that you made when you realized you didn't have the right ingredients tastes better than the original recipe. These wonderful surprises can make an otherwise pedestrian event a truly special occasion.

The good surprises have the added benefit of teaching you how to accept other unexpected turns in the road, even when they are less than delightful. You learn not to panic or pout. You learn how to pick up the pieces and reconstruct your expectations. You also discover that the unexpected adds a bit of spice to your affair.

Best case, you learn to have a sense of humor about all of the little twists and turns that can show up in the midst of your entertaining. The fact that we can't predict should be a delight to us, because it keeps us on our toes, carries us farther than our own imaginations, and teaches us important lessons about ourselves and others.

17.

Respect Your Guests

You have your own style and preferences, and you'll probably be the most successful host that you can be when you honor both. However, it's equally important to know and respect the styles and preferences of your guests. You don't have to be a chameleon to make subtle shifts in what you do and the way that you do it for the sake of your guests.

Consider, for example, if you plan to have music playing in the background when you entertain. Some styles of music do well for almost everyone, even if it isn't their first choice. Light jazz or popular classical music goes down fairly well with most adults without getting in the way of conversation or other competing noise. With a crowd who has in common an enthusiasm for a style of music, it may be just fine to go all out with country, R&B, sophisticated jazz, rock, or rap. The point is that you want the music to set a mood, not set nerves on edge.

Think, too, about how casual or formal you'll choose to be. It would be a shame to proclaim a "black tie" night with a group that included people who don't attend such occasions as a rule and don't own such apparel. Some people may be decidedly uncomfortable with eating on the sofa with plates in their laps, while others might find it pretentious to be served a multi-course meal with a table setting that includes a challenging set of silverware. You may have guests who would be put off by a pool party that required shorts and swimsuits.

If you know that you'll have both smokers and nonsmokers included in the party, be sure to provide a place for the smokers that keeps the nonsmokers comfortable, or make it clear (politely) that you prefer smokers to stand outside when they light up. In the same way, if you intend to serve alcohol, be sure to have nonalcoholic beverages available for those who don't or can't drink. Some hosts, and even their guests, choose to have an alcohol-free event for the sake of a recovering alcoholic. There's no rule of etiquette that says you have to go to such an extent, but courtesy certainly demands that you make it easy and comfortable for a guest to remain alcohol-free.

Respecting your guests—their tastes and choices—is a meaningful way to say that you care about them. Words are cheap, and even entertaining can be done with little regard to others. When you go to the trouble of knowing your guests and act on that knowledge with consideration and tact, you say something that words will never accomplish: "This is for you, because you are important to me."

18.

Forget Perfection

You don't have to be gloomy or pessimistic to acknowledge that perfection is an unrealistic goal that will lead to frustration and self-doubt. You only have to be in touch with life as it really is *for everyone*. Aiming for the best is all well and good. It gives you a worthy target that keeps you challenged. However, if your self-worth depends on always achieving the best that you can imagine, you'll set yourself up for a lot of needless pain.

Consider perfection as a yardstick against which you can measure the possibilities if you want, but don't let it become the measure of your failures. You have all of the qualities and abilities that you need to be a good host and offer your guests an enjoyable time with you. If you're willing to put in the work, you can do some remarkable entertaining that people will appreciate and remember. Will it be perfect, start to finish—all that you could hope or wish? Maybe once in a rare while it will be like that, but more often, there will be glitches and low spots that are impossible to avoid, but in the long run, far from disastrous.

Take a load off your mind and heart when you entertain. Get over the notion of perfection, once and for all. If you *could* achieve it consistently, your guests would feel inadequate and envious, and that's no fun at all. Join the human race in spirit, as well as in reality. Do your best, all the while knowing that you won't be perfect—and that's just fine.

19.

Measure Your Experiments

Entertaining can provide excellent opportunities for trying new ideas with food, music, activities, and combinations of people. With more people or a varied mix of people, you may be able to try food and activities that your partner or family wouldn't enjoy or appreciate. You can stretch your imagination and skills to attempt new culinary styles or improve old favorites with new touches. You can invite others to bring favorite music, wine, books, or desserts, and expand your horizons through their input. Any and all of your experiments can add zest and adventure to the business of entertaining.

In the interest of an enjoyable experience for all and a low level of stress for you, however, it's probably a good idea to create a reasonable mixture of new and old. Loading a single event with untried ideas gives you no "sure things" to fall back on, should your plans turn out differently than expected. In addition, the preparation is guaranteed to take longer when you're unfamiliar with what you're doing.

Having one or two labor-intensive items on your agenda is usually more than enough to keep you busy—but without overload or panic. You have the opportunity to test them in the safe context of elements that you are familiar with. Once you've tried them and know what you're doing, you can decide whether they're worth the effort and what you had hoped. Then for the next event, you can move on to other experiments and do the same.

You don't have to limit yourself in your entertaining. However, if you want to avoid the anxieties of labor and stress, measure out the experiments in small, easy-to-swallow doses.

20.

Anticipate Special Needs

You can alleviate a lot of hosting anxiety by knowing your guests and their needs ahead of time and making provisions for them. If you're entertaining people whom you haven't known for long or you don't know well, you only need to ask a simple question or two to judge what preferences you should take into account as you plan. By doing so, you eliminate unhappy surprises that can rob you of satisfaction and your guests of comfort or full participation.

Consider food issues. People deal with allergies, health issues, religious restrictions, and personal preferences when they eat. Your grilled steak, no matter how prime or perfect, will fall flat if you're serving a vegetarian or someone with serious cholesterol problems. Someone who can't tolerate dairy products will be the disappointed outsider when you serve up the cheese fondue or the homemade ice cream. Heaping on the goodies that people forswore for Lent or avoid because they follow a kosher diet could be almost offensive. Just ask, "Is there anything you can't eat or really dislike? I'm flexible, and I want you to have a great time!" If someone chooses to keep any dietary concerns or preferences quiet in the face of that, it is no longer your problem, and you can make your plans with confidence.

Think about any physical disabilities or limitations that your guests may have. A two-story party, a get-together that depends on active games, or one that requires people to do a lot of indoor/outdoor movement will be difficult for someone who has balance issues, is in a cast, or is sedentary in some other way. For those whose needs you know, make them aware when you invite them that you've already planned the perfect spot for them where they'll be comfortable and part of the action.

Remember that some people may have deathly allergic reactions to bee stings; may have difficulty breathing in the presence of certain allergens; may not tolerate heat or cold; or may have trouble hearing. This is not to say that you have to independently think and ask about this whole range of potential concerns. However, a good host knows these things in general, and will take them seriously if they come up. There's no need to obsess over what you may not know. Just be alert and sensitive, and your guests will know that you care about their comfort and well-being.

21.

Focus on Others

When you're the one entertaining others, it's easy to get caught up in how you'll be received or whether you'll be judged. You may worry about where you live, how you look, what you've planned, or any other of a dozen concerns. In fact, you can become so preoccupied with such issues that you miss out on the fun you have planned for others.

No better antidote for insecurity exists than a self-conscious effort to focus your attention on others. Forget about judgments, and think instead about who your guests are: the lives that they lead, the successes that they enjoy, or the frustrations that they battle. Give your attention to getting to know the people whom you entertain better. Ask questions about where they grew up, what they did as children, how they met their spouses or chose their careers, where they vacation, or even what they consider the perfect day. Aside from taking your mind off yourself, all of these topics make for lively, interesting conversation.

Find ways, as well, that your guests can have their moments in the limelight. If you're aware of something special or important in someone's life—a new grandchild, a special honor, an exciting opportunity—give that guest the chance to share it with others. You may simply acknowledge a bit of glory with a toast, which allows others to ask for more details or not, as the occasion seems to warrant.

Think about giving credit where credit is due, especially if your guests have contributed to the event in some way. Remember to say thank you for gifts, contributions of flowers, food, or drink, or any help given in the midst of the party. In fact, remember to thank your guests for coming. They gave up their time to be with you on your terms. It's a gift that bears noticing. You don't have to make a big production of it; simply remember to mention it in company. Not only will your guests feel appreciated, but you'll find yourself forgetting to worry about your own concerns. The net result will be a good time had by all—including you!

22.

Use Your Strengths

As adults, we understand that our self-worth does not depend on how we stack up in comparison to others. Your strengths may have to do with smarts, personality, physical coordination, imagination, background, training, or a great stew of all of these. No one is quite like you or has exactly the same mix of strengths as you. So when you set out to entertain, you bring to the enterprise a unique blend that makes your efforts as unique as you are. You may not be able to throw a party, host a dinner, or stage an event in the way that someone else does—and you don't have to.

When you entertain, focus on your strengths. Think in terms of what you do well, what you enjoy doing, and what others appreciate in you. Don't worry about whether the choices that you make echo the entertaining styles and choices of others. Conformity, although it is promoted and applauded in modern life, is a dim second cousin to originality. You don't have to try to be original. You are, by your very makeup and experience, one of a kind. Play to that, and make your mark one that reflects you.

23.

Build Traditions

All cultures have traditions. These are the repeated events, rituals, and perspectives that build a shared identity among families, clans, regions, religions, and nations. The traditions create a sense of belonging. They also establish regular opportunities to come together, to remember, to celebrate, and to move on as a group. Traditions are familiar and predictable, and that's part of what makes them comforting and enjoyable.

You can make your own traditions for entertaining, whether you focus on holidays, sporting events, changes of season, the anniversaries of your community, or some other occasion that you invent. A tradition may start with an event that turns out so well that everyone leaves saying, "This was great! We should do this every year!" It may be that you annually need to beat the blues when the dark days of winter descend, or you want to make the most of harvest season, or you have a special love of some benchmark day that you want to share with others.

Whatever the pretext, make the most of the "tradition" style of entertaining. Build on the sameness that people enjoy in traditions, and appreciate the fact that you don't have to keep inventing new ways of doing things. Let the predictability of the tradition work to your advantage by planning and preparing well in advance instead of dealing with the stress of a lot of last-minute work. Encourage others to take ownership of your traditional get-together so that they can be depended on, year after year, to make particular contributions.

On the other hand, don't let a tradition outlive its fun or get mired in a pattern that ultimately doesn't work for you. Everything in life is in a constant state of change. Traditions are just as changeable. Some people may bow out while new people join in. Some elements may work and some may not. Let the heart of the tradition live on while the clothes change.

Traditions, treated with respect and enjoyed for what they are, have the capacity to give you something to look forward to, year after year. They become cherished anchors in life that you have in common with people that you love and enjoy. Co-opt standing traditions or build your own. In either case, they will provide an event you can count on.

24.

Accept Help

Good manners dictate that guests offer a hand to the host during a social occasion. For some, politeness seems to dictate that the host demur, insisting that guests relax and enjoy one another while the host hustles. However, there's a missing piece in this scenario: Guests want to enjoy the company of their host, as well. While you're making multiple trips to the kitchen, rustling up extra chairs, or lighting candles, your guests are without you, and you're missing out on the conversation and festivities.

If you don't know it already, understand now that many—if not all—guests enjoy being of help. It's okay to take them at their word when they offer assistance. Depending on the guest and circumstances, you can even take the initiative and ask for someone's help.

First of all, think ahead to what simple, low-labor jobs you can hand out. Filling water glasses, lighting candles, passing trays, or schlepping dishes takes little work and time, but it draws guests into the action and brings them into proximity with you in the last minutes before a shared meal. Checking the grill or setting up the badminton net lets backyard company feel at home. Opening the wine, passing out napkins, showing a newcomer where to put his or her coat—all of these can be quickly accomplished and save you steps.

In addition, make a point of engaging your helpers in conversation. The best reason for soliciting help in the first place is the chance to have some one-on-one with a particular guest or to extend the party into the work area that you inhabit. If you simply hand out assignments and then doggedly go about your business, it's work. If you make yourself socially available in the midst of it, you make the helping part of the fun.

Finally, remember to say thank you. Gratitude is often in short supply, but its value cannot be overrated. Make a point of acknowledging help and expressing your appreciation for it.

25.

Invite Participation

Some sorts of help in social situations should not be solicited at the last minute. They require some thought or demand a bit of skill. To ask on the spur of the moment is to put a guest on the spot and potentially embarrass him or her. A little foresight is all it takes to invite the participation of your guests without sacrificing their sense that you are the one doing the host's job.

Ask ahead of time for assistance with such things as giving a toast, carving a roast, or asking a blessing before a meal. In the case of a big party, make greeting, grilling, or serving assignments well in advance. If you're hoping for people to share talents in music or storytelling, don't be spontaneous about it. Make it known when you issue invitations so that people have time to prepare.

Ask for participation that suits the actual skills and interests of particular guests. Is Joe known for grilling a hamburger to perfection? Joe's your man on the Fourth of July. Does Sheila have a way with words? She's the one to ask when you want a little speech. People enjoy opportunities to do what they do well—and everyone benefits.

Ask for participation that is actually meaningful to you. No one gets a charge out of "make-work," and few are fooled into thinking that it matters. If you're going to get people involved, the involvement should count in a way that is obvious to them and you.

Also remember to ask in such a way that people feel comfortable saying "no." It takes a light touch to pull this off, but you can say something akin to this: "I'm asking a few people to give a hand. I was wondering if you'd be able to help (don't say "willing"; no one wants to admit that they are not willing to help). *Please* feel completely free to pass on this. I'll enlist you another time." Most people will give an honest response in such a case.

People have a need to feel needed. Even when you're aiming to give people a treat, you can make their enjoyment richer by giving them a sense of participation. The better you know people, the easier you'll find it to invite appropriate participation—and the more others participate in your entertaining, the better you'll know them.

26.

Offer Alternatives

With the increasing awareness and emphasis on the importance of diet in relation to various health concerns, planning a meal for guests can be an exercise in juggling, at best. One person needs heavy doses of protein, another avoids meat, another hates fish, another eats foods only in prescribed combinations, and yet another is the original comfort food addict. What do you do?

One solution is to offer a meal that gives people options. When cooking a roast, for example, you can help make up the difference for a guest who is eating fat-free by providing a complement of vegetables that are substantial and tasty enough to serve in the place of a full-fat meat dish. If you intend to serve a heavy appetizer that is full of cheese and carbohydrates, include side dishes of vegetables cut for dipping and a low-calorie salsa for the dip. If you're presenting a rich dessert, decorate the table with bowls of fresh berries and tea biscuits for anyone who needs or wants something lighter.

If you know ahead of time the diets and preferences among your guests that will make the difference between a successful dinner and a disappointing one, do a little creative catering to individual tastes. Offering smaller portions of a greater number of dishes allows you to include more than one alternative for leaving your diners well-fed and happy. It doesn't need to cause a lot of extra work if you balance more labor-intensive dishes with simple, wholesome ones. You'll have the satisfaction of meeting your guests' needs where you find them, and giving them a treat that they can actually enjoy.

27.

Prepare for Surprises

O kay, so you think that it's in the nature and definition of a surprise that you can't prepare for it. In terms of the specific surprise, you're absolutely correct. You can't prepare for the fact that the garbage disposal will break during the dinner party, that an evening storm will offer a spectacular lightning display, that one of your guests will show up with two extra people, or that the florist will lose your order. Surprise, surprise!

How you respond to life's surprises, however, makes all the difference between having a good time anyway and losing your composure or suffering disappointment. Your responses in the face of surprise run primarily on autopilot. When the road you are traveling suddenly bends, you want to able to twist the wheel without thinking so as not to land in a ditch. Make up your mind to expect surprises, because life is full of them. The more you understand how inevitable surprise is, the more you can shrug and smile when it happens to you.

Even better—you can develop an appreciation for the way in which surprises enhance ordinary life. Even that broken garbage disposal in the midst of a dinner party offers something—if nothing else, a great story at a later time. If you look for what's ridiculous and humorous in the disasters, you can start chuckling when they happen. When nature's fireworks begin, you can call a halt to the action with your guests and let the power and beauty of the display become your unexpected entertainment. When the uninvited guests appear, you can see them as the unplanned spice you add to the party that you planned.

Your view of surprise largely determines your ability to respond in a positive way to it. Make a practice of noticing the value (including entertainment value) in surprise, and you'll find yourself well-prepared when it visits you.

28.

Prepare for Spontaneity

Spontaneity, like surprise, seems like something you can't prepare for. However, as with surprise, you can develop a receptive attitude to the *idea* of spontaneity that makes you more open to last-minute changes, unexpected plans, and spur-of-the-moment inspirations. With spontaneity, you gain a greater sense that things don't *have* to go the way you planned—or even have to *be* planned—in order for them to go well.

Begin to prepare for the spontaneous by thinking through what you would do "if": you had to put dinner on hold; your guests opted for a different movie than what you had in mind; the weather went south when people needed to drive; or someone's babysitter got sick. Simply rehearsing the possible ways in which you could switch gears in a pinch can make it easier to do so in reality.

The more you open yourself to last-minute changes, the less intimidating last-minute decisions become. That in turn can help you initiate spontaneous entertaining. You see an opportunity, seize it, and let the details sort themselves out. This has the great advantage of taking the pressure off how elaborate or involved your entertaining has to be. No one expects a big deal when an event is hatched on the spot. They don't expect your house to be spotless, the table to be set, the food to be gourmet, or the wine to be chilled. You can order out for pizza or Chinese food, and everyone says, "This is fun. Why don't we do this more often?"

Spontaneity requires that you accept what is. You don't have time to "do your homework." You can't control all the details. You have to face the event the way that you face life—as an organic wonder that sometimes proves that it has a will of its own, entirely outside of your control. This is good. Be prepared for it. Love it.

29.

Suit Yourself

You want your guests to enjoy your style of entertaining. That concept, however, shouldn't add more stress to your preparation. Consider the possibility that suiting yourself—making yourself happy in the way that you choose to entertain—may actually be the key to being the best kind of host you can be.

Go ahead and take the tastes and preferences of your guests into consideration when you plan how you will entertain them. Before you go too far down that road, however, think about your own individual style, and consider how it can work in the company of the people that you invite. Most people shine brightest when they know themselves and feel free to express who they are in the various things they do. This is no less true in the realm of entertaining.

What do *you* like? What makes you feel special and relaxed? If *you* were to design *your* idea of the perfect evening with friends, what would it look like?

Too often, we lay aside our intuition and ideas in deference to some exterior standard of what "people" do when they entertain—but people are as varied and quirky as the rest of the living world. They value authenticity, they enjoy originality, they are attracted to kindred spirits, and they have the ability to adapt. You can be yourself and entertain in a way that suits you and still have a reasonable expectation that the people you entertain will value what you have offered them.

30.

Plan to Rest

Preparations for entertaining often include planning that lasts up to the minute that you open your door to guests. If you organize the work that you need to do, you can sketch out a timeframe for the various items you need to take care of. Your schedule or to-do list will help you remember the last details and fit the work into the time you have.

Interestingly, many people have discovered that work tends to fill the time you give it. That is, if you have several hours to pull the meal together, you'll take several hours. If you're down to an hour and a half, you'll have the work done in that amount of time. In other words, your to-do list is likely to be accomplished in the time allowed.

What the host rarely gets is time to rest. Before playing host, why don't you catch a nap, take a bath, put your feet up, or take whatever form of rest most refreshes you? It rarely occurs to us to make this a "to-do" item, yet in terms of effective entertaining, it may be just as important as the last-minute straightening of the house or porch, the final touches on the hors d'oeuvres, or the loading of your CD player. Some of these jobs can, if needed, spill over into the time after your guests arrive. The one thing that you can't do in company is rest.

Consider the benefits of a short break in the action before you're "on." You have a chance to reenergize. You clear your mind sufficiently to think beyond the details of entertaining to the people that you're hosting—and you give yourself the resources to not only play the host, but to enjoy playing that role, as well. When you're making up the final list of what you need to do, remember rest, and schedule it in.

31.

Drecess for Comfort

By and large, the responsibilities of a host mean that, for the duration of your event, you are in motion at any moment and often on your feet. If you're throwing a volleyball picnic, that may not make you so different from your guests. Everyone is active, and you're all dressed for it. Athletic shoes and comfy casuals are the order of the day, and you can serve—in all respects—with ease.

The dress code for entertaining can range, however, from running shorts to formal attire, and may present far more of a challenge than an afternoon of active fun. For the sake of enjoying the entertaining that you do, it may be worth the time and money to choose a few outfits for host duty that bridge the gap between the business of serving and the level of formality that you've planned. Fashions vary at every level, and it's possible to answer the needs of both utility and style when you dress for guests.

Choose clothes that give you some freedom of movement. Whether or not you consciously notice it, confining clothes make you work harder, because you fight them with every reach and twist. If you're serving food, choose colors that are less likely to show the errant splatter, so that you don't have to waste emotional energy over wearing a stain or waste time changing clothes. Obviously, an apron will make you more comfortable in the kitchen, so if you don't have one that you feel happy wearing in company, get one.

Pay attention to your shoes. Tired feet are distracting and enervating. If you're used to high-fashion shoes that bear no resemblance to the natural shape and position of your feet, go ahead and wear them. However, the next time you're shoe shopping, notice the variety of styles that offer fashion *and* comfort, and consider whether these might be good options for at-home entertaining.

Clothes don't define the quality of your hosting, but they can have a definite impact on it. Choosing clothes that allow you to move in comfort will afford you a more relaxed and natural way with your guests, and everyone will have a better time.

32.

Avoid the Rush

A direct correlation exists between rush and stress. When you're entertaining and you leave a lot to remember and do at the last minute, you open the door to minor catastrophes that you'll have no time to fix, and you'll put yourself in a high-pressure mode that is hard to lose when the guests arrive. Before you know it, you're hurrying company along, and everyone feels the push.

You can avoid the rush by combining some common sense and some organizational work ahead of time. If you get home from work at six in the evening, for example, you're setting yourself up for stress if you plan to have your guests arrive at six-thirty. All it takes is an unexpected call, a traffic jam, or a bit of car trouble to put you in a true entertaining fix. If you have a three-day conference out of town, you'll make yourself frantic by inviting folks over for your first day back. If one of your kids has a major project due at school the day after your event, you create competition for time that you may want to have available to help your youngster.

If you know that time will be short at the last minute, be smart about what you plan. Choose dishes that thrive when frozen or stored so you can prepare food ahead of time. Prearrange help that can take some of the pressure off you in terms of being house- or garden-ready. Give thought ahead to what you'll wear, how you'll arrange your guests, and what you need to have on hand.

Don't let the trend toward overloading our schedules invade your personal life. Figure out the times that work for you and capitalize on them. Always give yourself breathing space between commitments, and teach yourself to think of the *total* time consumed by the kind of entertaining you plan. It's never just the event itself. You need to add in time for cleaning, shopping, preparing, and following up. Unless you know that you've got the time needed for all elements of the experience, you risk the rush that leads to stress.

33.

Go with the Flow

Imagine a stream flowing through the forest. On its surface floats a leaf. At times, the stream flows smoothly and calmly, and the leaf floats along at a pleasant, leisurely rate. There are also moments when river debris and rocks interrupt the smooth flow of the water, creating obstacles here and there in the forward motion. At other spots, a quick drop in the riverbed creates rapids and waterfalls. If the leaf travels with the flow of water, when it reaches an obstacle, it simply follows the current around the interruption. When the pace picks up and the water turns turbulent, it rides atop the froth and into the next stretch of calm without damage.

When you entertain, you follow a continuum of experience that can resemble that forest stream. All may go well for a while, and then suddenly, you face one or more obstacles to your plans. Someone can't make it until later than you want to begin; the dessert flops; your cable TV cuts out at halftime; or you burn yourself. You can get hung up on the obstacles, and let them interrupt the flow of either the event or your enjoyment of it. Alternately, you can make like the leaf, and go with the change of flow that the obstacles create. In the latter case, you commit yourself to having and making a good time of the event, regardless of the change in plans. You put people first and slide right by the rest of it.

Likewise, the even flow of your entertaining may bubble up when tempers flare, a guest drinks a little too much, someone touches on a sore subject, or someone becomes ill. If you let the turmoil suck you in, you'll lose your capacity to bring order and calm to the gathering. If you rise above it—skim the surface like the leaf—you can be the calm influence needed to preserve the good experience for your guests.

This mindset is often described as the "effortless effort." By temperament or training, you may find this an unusual approach to the bumps and excitements of entertaining, but it is an attitude that anyone can adopt to good effect. It eases the strain and serves everyone a dose of calm.

34.

Learn Your Lessons

Wisdom can be defined in a number of ways, but perhaps the most straightforward is "accumulated learning." When you entertain, you potentially deal with human beings, machines, logistics, and schedules. You have good experiences and bad experiences in every one of these arenas, and learn something about what works and what doesn't work. In fact, entertaining offers an abundance of learning experiences, if you pay attention and have a desire to grow.

Let experience aid you. For example, if a specific traditional event has come to be a chore, take an honest look at what makes it difficult. It may be the mix of people, whether it's a family affair or a regular event among friends. It may be the way that the work is distributed, the time of year that it occurs, or unacknowledged changes that have transpired since the tradition was first conceived. Whatever the problem, remember that you do not have to continue what does not work. You have choices, and the more you exercise them, the better.

Likewise, when you try something new in your entertaining and have less than positive results, give some thought to what went wrong. Pay attention to the specific ways in which your experience did not match your expectations and hopes. Take note of exactly why you felt disappointed. Then look for ways to save what worked while reshaping what didn't.

Note, as well, the combinations of guests that work and why, or conversely, the ones that don't. If you're giving a party, choose the people who mingle easily and add some life and interest to a large group. If you're having a one-on-one style of evening, invite the people who prefer a small, close gathering to a big event.

Most of all, always remember that you don't have to repeat bad experiences or mistakes. You can learn from past choices and choose differently. As you know better, you can do better.

35.

Offer Surprises

Offering your guests a helping of the unexpected can add a lot of life and enjoyment to an occasion. As much as many people love tradition and have perennially favorite events, they also can delight in surprises—elements that differ from the typical. When you plan surprises that reflect your special interests, talents, and preferences, you offer a piece of yourself in the process that can make your guests feel all the more welcome and appreciated.

Surprises can take as many forms as your imagination allows. There's the "do-it-yourself" surprise course—whether it's choose-your-own-topping mini-pizzas, a home-style smorgasbord, or a dessert "sundae bar"—that gives your guests the opportunity not only to pick and choose what they like, but also to exercise some creativity of their own.

Treat your guests to "reverse thank-you" gifts. Hand out miniature flower bouquets, nut breads, or candy samplers as they leave, or provide unusual napkin rings, place cards, or coasters and let your guests take theirs home. You can also give guests one-time-use cameras to use during the event, from which they can keep the photos that they've taken.

Consider rolling up the rug, pushing back the furniture, handing out clean socks, and throwing an impromptu "sock hop" to your favorite tunes after dinner. You could set up a soft horseshoe game using light flying rings and weighted plastic cups in the family room; an indoor croquet game with plastic golf balls, bats, and pairs of soda bottles as the wickets; or a game of carpet bocce, using plastic baseballs and empty plastic water bottles.

Obviously, some of these surprises require a bit of work, and all of them need advance planning. However, they can give you a leg up on keeping your gathering interesting and unusual, and you can be sure that your guests will remember the occasion with a smile.

36.

Make It a Gift

The business of inviting people into your life and home can sometimes offer a mixed bag of results. At one time or another, you will deal with problem people, meals gone awry, low energy, or a bad day. You'll encounter disappointments, frustrations, and aggravations. The question is, what perspective can you bring to bear that allows you to take satisfaction in your efforts, regardless of the results?

Perhaps one of the most effective ways of maintaining a positive attitude about what you've done as a host is to remember that at its core, entertaining is a simple gift to others. Even if you do not choose to give your guests something to take home, you make a gift of yourself, your hospitality, and your time when you invite them in. Their ability to receive your gift with grace does not reflect on you, but on them. The relative success of what you offer means less than the fact of the offer itself.

Any gift is a grace note in life. It is a voluntary offering to others that has the potential to brighten their lives. By definition, you don't receive compensation when you give a gift. When you think of entertaining as a gift, you let go of the expectation that you'll get something back for it. It's enough that you've done it.

Make a point of getting your mindset clear ahead of your event. From the first idea to the final cleanup, let your attitude be one of generosity. Think more about how you can make the event special, relaxing, or fun for your guests than about whether your efforts have been adequately appreciated or acknowledged. Understand that what people remember to say or do in response to your gift often does not reflect their actual feelings about it. If you are clear in your own mind that what you did was done as a gift, you can take pleasure and satisfaction without a lot of fuss from your guests.

37.

Be Bold

There was a time when assertiveness training was big business—probably because gender roles were undergoing some significant changes. People—especially women—needed support in assuming the new roles society allowed them. They had been programmed for so long to take a people-pleasing posture in relation to others that they hardly knew how to be themselves—or so the assertiveness training implied.

Times have changed, trends have moved on, and modern society has shifted away from the assertiveness talk that was so prevalent in the 1960s, 1970s, and 1980s. But the perspective that it represented is just as valuable and needed now as it ever was. People-pleasing as a relational style continues to tie many people into pretzels of anxiety. By definition, such an approach to relating requires that you submerge your own preferences and needs beneath the desires of others. It's only a matter of time before it takes a heavy toll.

When it comes to entertaining, the temptation to try to read the minds of others and make them happy, even at your own expense, can be a powerful force. It also has a high potential for exhaustion, frustration, and resentment. You cannot consistently deny your own ideas and well-being without a rising level of stress, and the more stress you introduce into your entertaining, the more the negative side effects infect your experience.

Do yourself a favor, and recognize the trap that people-pleasing inevitably becomes. The old adage that you can't please all of the people all of the time says it all. If you please one, you displease another. You can assume that at any given moment, someone in your vicinity is not happy about something. It may relate to you and it may not. Ultimately, however, it is their responsibility, not yours.

Be bold enough when you entertain to please yourself. Meet your own needs while planning to give others an enjoyable time. Take yourself into full account and make your peace with the fact that others will appreciate what you do more at some times than at others. If you can at least please yourself, you'll know that someone is happy.

38.

Be Gentle

Boldness—the courage to be, do, and say what you want—does not have to lead to unkindness or lack of courtesy toward the people you entertain. You may not be able to make others happy all of the time—especially when you commit yourself to caring for yourself—but you can certainly take their feelings into account. A gentle touch smooths the edges of assertiveness and makes it palatable for everyone.

You can handle people gently by letting them know what to expect when you entertain them. Advance notice of dress code, food style, who else is invited, and what they can contribute gives people a greater comfort level and sense of security. By giving them a basic heads-up on the details, you allow them to prepare themselves and arrive confident and ready to be part of what you have planned.

You can also exercise a gentle touch by being a careful observer and good listener in regard to your guests. If you pay attention, it's usually not that difficult to figure out when a guest feels ill at ease for one reason or another. A little extra attention will go a long way toward putting a person back into the comfort zone without a lot of fuss.

When a guest inadvertently launches disaster—spilling a full glass of wine, knocking over and breaking a fragile item, saying the wrong thing to the wrong person—gentleness can make up the difference. Make a point of being the person who makes a molehill of any mountain, communicating clearly that your primary concern is the welfare of your guest, not the smooth motion of your occasion. Beware of teasing or joking in such a situation, unless you know the person well. Generally, diverting the attention of others and clearing the rubble as quickly as possible is the kindest, most effective way to relieve your offending guest of anxiety and embarrassment.

Gentleness requires just a little effort and pays big dividends. It allows you to be yourself while honoring the needs and feelings of your guests. It keeps your entertaining on an even keel and makes up the difference when you have thoughtless guests. Make it a point to be a gentle host whose courtesy and kindness make people glad that they said "yes" to your invitation.

39.

Depersonalize Disappointments

When you entertain, you put your ego on the line, even if it's only to a minor degree. It shouldn't surprise you, then, if your feelings are easily hurt by upsets and insensitive behavior from your guests. You invest enough of yourself that it's hard not to take it personally when things go awry.

You'll do yourself and your guests a big favor if you can learn not to make a personal issue of every glitch in the occasion. If your invitation is turned down, give the invitee the benefit of the doubt. If someone fails to respond to an RSVP on time, make up the difference by placing a call yourself rather than fuming at their lack of courtesy. If people arrive late, leave early, have trouble doing things your way, or get pushy with their own ideas, chalk it up to their peculiarities rather than taking it on the chin as a blow.

People have such differences in the ways they've been raised and trained that it's hard to know whether they operate from the same social rulebook as you. To read differences as a personal affront is to greatly overestimate the degree to which people are aware of how others interpret their behavior and choices.

When you're faced with guests' behavior that insults you in some way, seek first to understand what's behind what they've said or done. If you can't understand—if you can find no excuse for their behavior—you still have a couple of choices. You can choose to overlook the offense and move on in the confidence that it was unintentional, or you can actually confront the person, without rancor or undue emotion, and ask for clarification.

Every once in a rare while, a guest may actually behave badly and mean it personally against you. The best that you can say in such a case is that you have identified someone whom you do not need to invite again. Knowing this allows you to let the perceived offense roll off your back. It also teaches you a valuable lesson on how it feels to be hurt. This in turn will help you to be more sensitive to others yourself.

40.

Tolerate Others' Idiosyncrasies

We all have our little foibles and oddball habits—some of them not so little and some of them very odd. If we get involved socially with others, there's every reason to believe that these things will show up in company, just as surely as they do in more private situations. However, the truth is that the strange behaviors and habits of individuals—all those ways in which we don't fit the mold—are part of what makes the company of other people most interesting. So why is it that we hold it against one another when our idiosyncrasies come to the surface?

The next time one of your guests acts out his or her individuality in some kooky way, take a step back from irritation or anxiety. When Charlie picks his teeth, Kelly tells her too-long story, or Mabel insists on resetting the table *her* way, be the one who takes it in stride. Pat the belcher on the back and say, "That's a compliment in some countries. You're welcome." Offer the fussbudget some extra attention. Be the one who turns on the upstairs television for the antsy sports fanatic on game night.

As host, you set the tone for everyone's reaction to the unusual behavior of a particular guest. People will follow your lead if you choose to put a tolerant spin on your guests' behavior. Even if in your heart of hearts, you are vowing never to entertain that nutcase again, you can make the moment more comfortable and enjoyable by accepting each guest as he or she is.

Most idiosyncrasies are far from dealbreakers in friendship. They are simply what the term implies—the peculiar habits of people who have streaks of the individual in them. They often add humor and richness to a gathering. They either break up the monotony of the predictable, or—in the case of people who know one another well—lend a sense of continuity to your camaraderie.

All in all, it's the strange stuff of human nature that keeps us laughing and curious. Give it its due when guests call, and you'll have a good time.

41.

Know Your Space

Knowing and accepting the real limits within which you live and entertain takes a lot of the strain out of both your choices and experiences. Rather than frustrating yourself with plans that overreach your resources, you deal with the realities and suit what you do to what you have. One of the many factors that you need to take into account when you entertain is the space that you have available in which to do it. Like it or not, there is an absolute limit to what will safely and comfortably fit in any given space. If you're entertaining at home, you have a finite number of seats for people to sit in. Unless you invite people who are both willing and able to sit comfortably on the floor or stand, you need to consider where you are going to put everybody.

If you want to use porch or deck space for anything more than an intimate gathering, take the time to have an expert check out the safety limits. Every year, the media carries stories of needless tragedies that began as good times but loaded too much weight onto an inadequate structure. Close the door to any area that isn't up to the strain of what you plan.

If you intend to cook when you entertain, you need to consider the capacity of your kitchen. People with tiny kitchens often get around the limitations of that by bringing in food from outside sources or serving only food that can be prepared ahead and adequately stored until serving time. The lack of oven space may dictate an emphasis on cold food. A small refrigerator may require the use of ice chests for food, cold beverages, ice, or storage platters on a smaller than average scale. The absence of a dishwasher may suggest the informality of paper plates and cups.

Also think ahead about the availability of parking. Some neighborhoods or driveways can handle quite a number of cars, but if parking will affect neighbors, it's always diplomatic to let them know ahead of time and make sure that your guests won't be a burden. If space is very limited, it may be a good idea to find the nearest commuter parking lot and suggest that people carpool to the house. Any number of solutions can be found to parking limitations, but forethought takes the worry out of it.

Space limits of whatever sort do not need to cramp your entertainment style. Just adjust the scale and details to suit what you have, and your guests will enjoy themselves in whatever space is available.

42.

Take It Away from Home

Depending on the location and scale of your home, some kinds of entertaining may simply not work. In that case, depending on what you aim to do, you will find plenty of other venues that can provide what you need. A little online or phone-book research will give you all of the information that you need to plan an away-from-home event.

Some people go so far as to book a block of rooms, suites, or cottages for an overnight or more with a large group. Extended families, groups of friends with a common interest, or long-term vacation buddies can create an event that lasts for days without any one family or individual carrying the burden of providing the facilities. This works best in financial terms if everyone is willing and able to pitch in. Some resorts and hotels offer better rates to a group booking a block than they do to people getting individual rooms. Some of the food and fun can be contributed by the guests, as well, keeping the overall cost to the host down.

Many restaurants have rooms available for parties, if you reserve ahead. This is an excellent solution to the large parties associated with special events such as graduations, weddings, baby showers, and other benchmarks in life. Facilities also exist that are designed specifically and solely for large private gatherings. You can make such a place your own by working with the people who run it and adding touches that reflect who you are and what you prefer. Make sure that you know ahead of time how much flexibility you have so you don't spin your wheels with plans that will have to be abandoned.

Outside entertainment can be greatly improved by moving it to a park that has facilities and attractions unavailable at home. Here again, make sure you do your homework. Find out what fee you might have to pay to reserve space, a pavilion, or a given number of barbecue grills. Ask about bringing your own grills, alcoholic beverages, sports equipment, or music. Check ahead before you show up with a clown show or a pony. No one wants the last-minute embarrassment of a police officer or park official shutting down your fun.

Home limitations don't have to define your entertaining. You may need to do a bit more work to arrange your event when you do it away from home, but you will take the stress out of your space and facility worries.

43.

Err on the Side of Plenty

Perhaps one of the more unnerving situations that a host can face is running out of provisions before a party is over. Whether you're serving snacks, cocktails, a meal, or dessert, you want to know that everyone had as much as they wanted before they left your event. You can easily take the worry out of your entertaining on this score by planning to have plenty right from the beginning.

One good rule of thumb is to know your guests and their eating habits. If you're serving someone with a notably big appetite, count that person as two people when you prepare food. If you have an absolute limit to an expensive element in a meal—most often the meat—make sure that you have an extra quantity of the other dishes so that no one has to stop short of full. Always offer some "fillers" such as bread and relish trays so that people have plenty to chew on. Plan at least two extra servings of any sort of food or drink.

When you're planning a party, choose at least some food items that will save well after the party is over. Such items can be made in larger-than-necessary quantities, because the leftovers will not be wasted.

If you expect a big crowd or have any doubts about how many people will actually show up, you may want to stock some pantry items that can be brought out in a pinch. Many unusual "gourmet" items are now available in a nonperishable form, so don't neglect this backup.

Don't worry about having enough when you entertain. Plan to have more than enough. It never hurts to be overstocked.

44.

Choose Your Occasions

If you've done any sort of traditional entertaining over a number of years, you may feel locked into continuing what you've done in the past. No one likes the feeling of being trapped. Unless you love every minute of it, just knowing that a certain event or a certain way of doing things is "expected" by others is enough to cause stress. As long as you continue to fulfill such expectations against inner objections, you will continue to experience the stress.

It's important to understand that you are making a choice in such a situation. You may *feel* trapped, but in fact, no one can force you to do what you've done before. They may put a lot of pressure on you, but you are the one who either caves in to that pressure or does not.

Accept the fact that you need to take care of you. Only you can determine when the time is right for you to entertain and what that entertaining will look like. Only you will know when the "expected" is too much to expect of you. Only you will know when you're ready, willing, and able to go all-out on an occasion.

Don't allow history or pressure from others to be your guide. Be the captain of your own fate by making a conscious "yes" or "no" choice about each occasion when you choose to entertain. It's a copout to blame others for the choices you make—so don't do it.

When you care for yourself first, you're like the airline passenger who puts an oxygen mask on him- or herself before trying to help others. Only then do you have the inner resources to offer, freely and with good will, your home, energy, and self to others.

45.

Treat Family Like Friends

All of us form patterns of relating early in our lives. The habits and dynamics of our childhoods often stick, especially in regard to our family members. No matter how grown up we become, no matter how much we learn and grow, when we're plunked down in the midst of family, we turn into the childhood versions of ourselves. This can make for some built-in stresses when it's time to entertain family.

When you face the prospect of family entertaining, remember first and foremost that the dynamics of childhood are simply habits of the past. You do not have to relive childhood every time the family gets together. Habits are made, and habits can be broken. The first step to breaking old habits is acknowledging them for what they are—vestiges of something that no longer exists. You're not the kid sister or brother stuck in the same house with a bothersome sibling; you no longer live under the control and at the mercy of judgmental parents; and you are not a child. In the most important respects, you get to call the shots in your adult life.

So how do you break free of those old, not-so-pleasant family habits when you're entertaining the gang? Start by taking a brand-new look at your family members. Step out of the past, and reckon with the ways that they, just like you, have changed with age. Consider the hardships that they've had to endure and the challenges that they face in their present lives. Take note of their accomplishments and achievements. Give credit where credit is due for their growth and development.

Next, compare the way that you think and behave with family to how you are with friends. What differences do you notice? How would your friends feel if you gave them the same treatment? Are the differences built on issues from the past, or do they truly reflect the present reality?

With the new vision and perspective that such reflections offer, consider ways in which you can treat your family members as you would treat valued friends. Think of the kindness, good humor, compassion, and generosity that come easily in reference to friends, and transfer those qualities to the people of your childhood. Their response is not the issue. What matters is who and what you are with them. Remember, it always takes two to create an atmosphere, for better or worse. If you change, the people around you will have to change, as well.

46.

Treat Friends Like Family

Whatis it about family that makes people without family look on with envy and longing? The answer to that question probably differs from one person to the next, but a few of the basic ingredients of family certainly account for some of its attractions.

Probably the most fundamental aspect to what makes family alluring is a sense of belonging. Family members may like one another or they may not. They may have great times together or do a lot of fighting. The one thing that remains the same is the fact that they share ties of blood, history, memories, and ancestors. Other people may come and go from a person's life, but family remains.

A particular comfort level exists in family, as well, born of the years spent in intimate contact with one another. Customs, traditions, habits, quirks, mannerisms, and physical characteristics—all of these make for a certain automatic comfort zone among family members. You know what to expect, and that's comforting.

Families also enjoy a shared vocabulary. This is more than just the vernacular of a particular ethnic group or geographical region. Certainly, you and your birth family share such a language base, but you also share a vocabulary of mutual experiences—the reference points inherent in nicknames, inside jokes, the characters and stories of books, the lyrics of songs, pets, vacations, and so forth. These help you communicate with one another in a shorthand fashion that can be delightful.

All of this adds up to a mutual knowledge and understanding that is hard to beat—and in some important ways, it does not have to be confined to family. When it comes to entertaining, you can add a growing dimension of pleasure by building some of the same positive elements into your gatherings of friends that you have with family.

When you choose a group of people to gather regularly and express the pleasure that you derive from them, you imbue a sense of belonging that can be almost as rewarding as family. The more often you get together with specific people—and especially when you let everyone pitch in—the greater the comfort level you develop. Likewise, as you accumulate shared experiences of various sorts, you learn a common vocabulary that creates a shorthand and adds a comforting quality to your interaction. Take the best of what family represents and make your friends the family that you get to choose.

47.

Be Where You Are

People who deal professionally with stress, its sources, and its cures seem to agree that one of the most common causes of stress in daily life is multitasking. The experts have documented higher blood pressure, higher levels of adrenaline, increased heart rate, impaired concentration, chronic overeating, and excess alcohol consumption as typical symptoms of multitasking.

You might say that some aspects of life demand multitasking, and you'd be correct. Certainly, entertaining demands the ability to juggle jobs and concerns. Many of the same experts who identify the problem of multitasking offer some pointers on a solution. At the heart of the cure is the ability to be wholly where you are.

What does this mean? Most notably, it means that in the midst of your dinner party, you lay aside your internal struggles with tomorrow's conference call, yesterday's fight with your spouse, what you didn't get done, or what a mess you'll have to clean up later. Instead, you plant yourself firmly in the moment. You pay attention to what is, right now, and give your entire consciousness to being in the moment and in the event.

Give yourself the health and enjoyment benefits of concentrating on entertaining when you invite guests. Take note of the times when your thoughts drift or your attention is distracted. If you need to, quickly jot down reminders of the thoughts that are nagging you so that you can let them go in the present moment without fear of forgetting. Come back to them at leisure—after your guests leave. Meanwhile, consciously turn your attention to your guests and their needs, the fun that you're having, and the details of the event. You'll be amazed at how the stress level sinks.

48.

Share Yourself

Most of us want to know that we have something special to offer, whether we're entertaining, working, volunteering, or simply taking part in family life. When we entertain, though, the pressure to produce a one-of-a-kind event is not only unrealistic; it's shortsighted and stressful.

Great parties, gourmet meals, and fabulous entertainments sound appealing and add real zip to life, but they tend to be time-consuming and expensive, and for some of us, they are exercises in frustration. We either don't have the resources, or we lack the know-how or background to really pull them off.

When you consider the ways in which you can make your entertaining special to your guests, keep in mind that there's one thing you bring to the mix that will never be reproduced by another host, and that's *you*. When you bring *yourself* to your guests, you offer them something that they won't find anywhere else.

When you entertain, resist the temptation to get so caught up in the various details of the event—the hands-on work of entertaining—

that you become unavailable to your guests. Just like your company, you have stories to tell and listen to; you relate to others in ways that add meaningfully to the mix of people and personalities. It's wonderful to share your resources and your home with others, but it's even grander to share yourself. *You* are the single most important factor to hosting an original gathering—one that people won't find anywhere else.

49.

Share Your Heritage

One of the great virtues of modern life is the extent to which people of a wide variety of ethnicities, nationalities, and belief systems have come together to work and live. Most modern cities and their suburbs include people from all over the world, with all of the fascinating variations of style, food, and customs in their background.

Where do you come from? What elements of your life reflect the specific influences of your family and your ancestors? Even for people with a mix of backgrounds in their own bloodline, there tend to be distinctive traits that have arrived via family.

When you entertain, consider whether your heritage may offer some rich and textured possibilities as you choose refreshment, music, activities, or venue. On a cold winter's evening, a "Mom's comfort food" theme can give everyone an opportunity to revisit childhood by contributing a favorite from their own experience. At a holiday that your ethnic group celebrates in an unusual way, you can offer others a taste of your own world that will enrich theirs. If your gathering includes people with various customs related to one season, you can concoct an event at which everyone gets to share a little bit of their own.

Tensions exist all over the world between people of different backgrounds. Some of the conflicts arise out of political and economic struggles that have existed over hundreds or thousands of years—but some of it comes from ignorance and prejudice. People lack an up-close, sympathetic, and open exchange of ideas. When you know and care about a specific person, his or her differences become more intriguing than frightening.

Maybe your entertaining won't change the geopolitical problems of the day, but if you freely share your own heritage and invite others to do the same, you may contribute to your local community. At the same time, you'll have an opportunity to celebrate the variety that exists within the human race.

50.

Look for Simple Solutions

It's easy, when you entertain, to let the pressure of hosting others tempt you into overkill. You have a set of concerns and a list of desires that you need to satisfy in order for your planned event to go as you want, and because you will have an audience, you overdo. Your self-esteem and pride are on the line.

Unfortunately, the hyper approach to dealing with the details of entertaining tends to backfire. You make yourself overtired, stressed, and anxious trying to create perfection on every level, and in the process, you increase the odds of disaster. Too many big-deal aspects of the single event make it a mountain to climb.

When you find yourself bogging down under a load of preparation and decisions, take a giant step back and breathe deeply. Remember, there's no way that every one of the details that you're dealing with carries an equal level of importance for the success of your plans. Look carefully at what you are doing, and identify the one or two main focuses of your entertaining. It is in these that you want to invest your primary energy and resources.

As to the rest of the details, once you nail down what you care most about, look for simple solutions to the lesser items. Keep in mind that as you orchestrate your event, you set the stage for what your guests will focus on. If you make too much of everything, most of that hard work will be lost on the people you entertain. They literally won't know where to look. If instead you give your best to the main attraction, whether it's food, flowers, activities, or something else, they'll not only appreciate your efforts but also will get the greatest enjoyment out of it themselves.

Learn how to measure your fussing so that you can concentrate on what's significant. Everyone gains when you can sort out the trivial from the important—especially you.

51.

Delight in Your Guests

When you entertain, you are, for the most part, the master of your fate. As host, you determine the guest list. You have the final say not only on who will be invited, but on how many and in what combination. Granted, some of your entertaining may be on behalf of your spouse's or your professional life, or you may be host to an affair with certain obligatory invitees. Still, you have primary responsibility for the people involved.

Remember as you greet your guests at the door that attitude is everything in life. You may or may not like the people that you have invited, depending on the event. You may or may not find them intrinsically interesting or engaging. However, the way that you respond to them is completely within your power to control.

In the interest of everyone having the best possible time, why not make up your mind in advance to find delight in every one of your guests? Take satisfaction in their presence. Look for what is worthy and enjoyable in each of them. Let curiosity and a sense of humor make up the difference with people who tend to bring out negative emotions in you. Appreciate the contributions of those who fall on your positive side.

Once you make up your mind to look at each and every person as a piece of work—whether you define that as a masterpiece or a case to crack—you have the opportunity to truly enjoy the experience of being with them. When you respond to them with positive energy, you bring out the best in them and discover new facets to them. You quickly discover that behind even the most stubborn or outrageous demeanor lurks a person just like you, hungry for acceptance and hoping for a meaningful part to play in this life. Sometimes, where you least expect it, you'll find a kindred spirit and a true friend.

52.

Win Them with Love

The accoutrements of entertaining can easily take on dispropor-
tionate importance in a host's thinking. We invest so much of
our time, attention, and resources in food, drink, and other
amusements that we begin to believe that they really will create the
difference between a great time for our guests and a bust.

Think back, though, to your own experiences as a guest, rather
than as a host. When did you have the best time? What gave you
the greatest pleasure? What most consistently provided happy
memories that have never disappeared? If you're like most people,
your finest memories of good times as a guest revolve around
occasions when you felt loved and appreciated by your hosts, when
you knew that you were wanted and enjoyed. The accoutrements
meant little in comparison, because you felt that you were important
to the people who hosted you.

Now put the shoe on the other foot, and consider where you are
investing your greatest energy when you entertain. Think about

113

what happens when you wear yourself out with preparations and overburden yourself with the work of preparing, serving, and behind-the-scenes fixing. You get so involved with the logistics and extras that you can't give your best to the people. Meanwhile, your guests do without the cues from you of whether or not you're glad to have them.

Think first of how to make your guests feel loved. Give them plenty of the "warm fuzzies" that assure them that they are wanted, enjoyed, and treasured by you. If you do, you can be sure that they'll find whatever else you do to simply be frosting on the cake of a warm, welcoming experience.

53.

Plan for a Good Mix

Some great get-togethers happen entirely by serendipity. A chance overlap of people turns out to be a fabulous mix of interests and personalities, and without effort, you suddenly feel like the host with the most. People are having a blast, and you're reaping the credit and reward for really knowing how to put a shindig together.

Most of the time, however, it takes a little more thought and care to combine people. Yet it's as worth the effort to mix people well as it is to coordinate food, music, or décor. Even when all of the people involved are goodhearted, well-meaning folk, some combinations will work better than others.

It always adds interest to include a mix of viewpoints in a gathering where people will be inclined to exchange ideas. Although the comfort level tends to be high when everyone agrees, a bit of unpredictable give-and-take does no harm. You may want to think twice about putting people together who hold strong views in total opposition to one another, unless you have some skill at finessing a heated debate. Just don't feel obliged to stick to combos with matching ideas. That can be about as drab as a meal of only one food. A whole plate of cooked carrots is nutritious and tasty, but it sure is dull.

Think, too, about bringing people together from different neighborhoods. The traditional block party has a lot to commend it—it builds community and esprit de corps, if handled well—but there's nothing like new blood among familiars to wake people up. Old news and information suddenly become interesting again, and the overall energy level almost automatically picks up.

Don't be afraid to mix up the generations, either. Every generation has its contribution to make. Children bring a sense of play and adventure that older folks can easily lose. The elderly, given half a chance, offer a lifetime of perspective, wisdom, and understanding that has been earned by sheer survival. People in the midst of life are full of what's going on and what they have to do with it.

Critical to the good mix is you, the host, making sure that people receive helpful clues to launching conversations with people that they haven't met before or don't know well. Once you've got them going, you may be surprised at the momentum the interaction will gather. Don't waste your entertaining on what feels safe or comfortable all of the time. Take the chance on a new, good mix of guests.

54.

Avoid Rumination

We all have past events and situations that stick with us, either because they impressed or delighted us, or because they had a negative impact that we have never managed to shake. These pieces of our personal histories, when they are positive, give us fuel for the present and future. They build our confidence and hope. When they are negative, they leave a residue of doubt and anxiety.

You may have memories from your experiences as a host that have left their imprint on you, for better or worse. The good memories are worth holding on to. You can build on those experiences to become a more skilled and relaxed host. You can take what you learned about particular people and how they interact to create future guest lists. You can fill some of your quiet moments with happy recollections.

The bad memories, on the other hand, are best forgotten. Certainly, you can and should learn from negative experiences. Some ideas don't work. Some meals turn out badly. Some people make disappointing guests. Some plans are too elaborate or ill-conceived to work. When your entertaining fizzles, go ahead and figure out what went wrong. When you've finished your assessment, however, it's time to wash away the bad taste that the experience left in your mouth.

You can't change what is done and gone. If you have apologies to make, make them. If you have someone that you need to forgive, do it. If you have lessons to learn, put yourself to the task, and learn the lessons. Understand that ruminating—chewing, rechewing, and chewing again—does nothing but leave an unpleasant lump in your throat that can steal your confidence and perpetuate bad feelings. Let the past slip into the past. Every day is a new day, and it's never too late to do better than you have in the past.

55.

Think Small

Do you find the idea of a big party or a large group of people intimidating? Do the logistics of handling a crowd send you into a panic? Does your mind boggle over the weights and measures involved in feeding the herd? Don't work yourself into a sweat. Even the largest gathering can be managed in such a way that you can overcome your reservations. As with so many of life's challenges, it has to do with how you view it.

Consider first that there's absolutely nothing wrong with having small groups when you entertain. There's no law that says that everyone must host a large event at some point in life. If you're the small-do type, give yourself to the enterprise with joy and confidence. Don't give a thought to what you are *not* doing—that is, having the big gig of the century. Take pride and pleasure in what you *are* doing.

If you want to venture into deeper water but lack confidence to do it, start on the small side and work your way up a bit at a time.

There's little to choose between two guests and four, four and six, and six and ten. All it takes is some multiplication. Once you get up to twelve people, you might as well be dealing with twenty. Try adding just a few from one event to another, and see how easy it becomes. By the time you go back to two, it may seem paltry.

Meanwhile, as you consider how to arrange or feed people, keep in mind that people in a crowd never or rarely relate to the entire group. You can count on people to subdivide themselves into manageable, smaller groups. When you think of how to present appetizers, for example, think in terms of numerous small dishes and scatter them about, where a number of small conversation groups can gather to schmooze and nibble. Set up serving stations for a full-course dinner, and let people help themselves buffet-style before finding seating throughout your entertainment area. If you have a variety of dishes, you'll find that people rarely take full portions of any one dish, which means that you can make less than a mountain of each.

As you plan your party, break the preparation into manageable, small stages. Bit by bit, you can tick off the items on your list without the sense that you've hung a millstone around your neck. No matter how big a bang you want to make, you'll need to do the work one step at a time. Work out the steps and start doing them. Before you know it, your big party will be in full swing with a happy host at the helm.

56.

Think Seasonally

Don't let the choices involved in entertaining make you crazy!
If where to have your guests, what to feed them, what
activities to provide, or what decorations to use leave you in a
muddle, take a natural approach to theme and style. Let the season
be your guide.

There's more to "season," of course, than spring, summer, fall,
and winter. Those categories give you a good starting place, but
"season" also has to do with sports, holidays, customs, and
particular harvests. You can pin a party of whatever size on any sort
of season you prefer. By working with a natural, given set of
parameters, you'll simplify the business of creating your event.

One of the great benefits of thinking seasonally is the
availability of decorations and ingredients that match your theme.
You can obtain the food and drink that people expect and
appreciate. You can readily find the colors and accoutrements that
suit. This doesn't mean that you can't add your own original twists,

but you won't be hunting in vain for flowers in the right spectrum, foods in the complementary flavors and textures, or music to match the seasonal mood.

It's all very well to think that a "summer-in-winter" party would give everybody a lift or a laugh. It can be a lot of fun, and if you have the time, patience, and resources to pull it off, more power to you. However, if you're hoping to make your life easier and lessen the stress of entertaining, you'll be better served by planning within the range of the season—whatever your definition is for that. You're likely to discover that your guests in no way find the fixings trite or unpleasant, and you'll be far more rested and relaxed for having concentrated on what you can find at your fingertips.

57.

Share the Planning

No one ever said that entertaining has to be a solo performance. In fact, many occasions present a natural opportunity for sharing the planning with others. In the process, you create allies and helpers to ensure the success and enjoyment of what you plan.

Look for the times when an outside focus gives you and your guests a common cause. Someone's birthday, a graduation, anniversary, new house, or new baby in the family can create an occasion that just begs for sharing the credit (and work) for planning a party among friends. It's a chance for a number of people to show their love and appreciation while taking some of the planning load off the host.

Since you're the one who's actually hosting, you can act as "chair" of your planning committee. You know what your resources and facilities can handle, and taking the leadership position allows you to have the final say on arrangements that affect or strain either. You also have the ability, in such a case, to take charge of who will work with you to plan. There may be people with whom you find it easier to coordinate than others. In fact, there are probably people who you enjoy so much that involving them in the planning will make it as much fun as the party itself.

Keep in mind that sharing implies that you truly delegate—you actually hand over some jobs and decisions to others. When you do, you free yourself to give more energy and imagination to the aspects of the planning that you retain for yourself. It helps to share the planning with people that you know and respect sufficiently to trust their judgment and depend on their follow-through. If you're dealing with a loose cannon in any respect, you may find yourself more stressed in sharing the load than you would have been in handling the entire planning yourself.

Some occasions are good "group projects." Others either do not warrant that level of involvement or they become more involved than they're worth by the time you try to bring others into planning them. Choose your entertainment moments for this sort of help. It will spread the fun, the work, and the investment, all of which can only enhance the overall event.

58.

Share the Preparation

The success of a social occasion often owes at least as much to good preparation as it does to the happening itself. Just as you don't have to carry the full load of planning for an event by yourself, you can likewise choose to share the preparation. When you plan to entertain, even on a small scale, consider whether you might be able to increase the fun and cut the work for yourself by inviting your guests to get involved.

Many groups of friends who gather regularly make it a practice to distribute advance food preparation—an improvement on the old-style potluck. They divide up the courses of a dinner, giving each guest responsibility for just one part of the meal. If you as host want to be sure that the parts of the meal work well together, you may choose to assign not only the category of food—vegetable, salad, appetizer, dessert, and so forth—but also the ingredients. However you choose to make your advance food assignments, you will cut your own food preparation at least in half, making for a more relaxed occasion where you can give quality attention to people instead of food service.

If you're entertaining on the fancy side and have some ideas for decoration that will take time, consider drawing others into the work. If your guest list includes a couple of close friends, invite them over for wine, cheese, and napkin-folding days in advance; or take a pal or two on your supply run and cap it off with lunch out; or barter for help with a friend who has a big gig coming up, as well.

If you like the idea of sharing preparation, consider making the food preparation itself the focus and highlight of your entertainment. Many meals have the potential to be an on-the-scene group activity, especially if they involve a lot of chopping, multiple last-minute steps, or "create-your-own" features. Individual pizzas, tostados and tacos, salad meals, a sundae bar for dessert, or even a cookie-making party all allow for group participation that is not only fun but delicious.

Sharing the preparation for entertaining offers enjoyable moments with friends and family. It also gives your entertaining a richer texture, as different guests or contributors add their own special touches. Just be sure to check in advance that everyone is happily on board with your idea, and give guests the heads-up in terms of what they need to wear or bring (such as aprons). Then belly up to the kitchen counter with your pals, and be thankful for their company and help.

59.

Take It Outside

Just about everyone has enjoyed a good holiday picnic or neighborhood volleyball game when the weather is fine and the occasion presents itself. The outdoor venue gives an expansive feel to a gathering that's hard to match indoors, and it's often possible to accommodate a larger group without the usual constraints of four walls.

Outdoor entertaining does not need to be limited to the typical summer lawn party, however. If you and your intended guests have a love of the outdoors in common, give some thought to expanding the times and places in which you take advantage of that. Every season has potential, if you watch for it. Ice skating or an après-ski bonfire and food on spits can really warm up a winter afternoon. An apple feast staged in an apple orchard or pumpkin field, or a "new wine" and cheese party at a vineyard not only gets you outside, but it also offers a "taste of the season" that creates warm memories. Autumn and winter can be the best seasons for hiking through woodlands that, in season, become impassable with undergrowth and rife with biting insects.

Consider spring adventures in bird-watching, a first-planting garden party, or a boat outing on a river or lake to view spring's new leaves and flowers. Even a walk in a soft April shower can allow you to take your guests outside after a filling meal.

In an age when most people spend large portions of their week indoors at work, travel from one place to another in closed cars, and routinely make television and movies their "down time" amusement, finding ways to be out-of-doors may seem like a challenge. Getting outside has the potential to let you and your guests regain a sense of life's natural rhythms, to draw deep breaths of fresh air, and involve all of your senses in having a good time.

60.

Make It a One-Course Event

Sometimes, the simplest events are the most fun for everyone, host and guests included. When you choose to host a one-course get-together—appetizers, dessert, tea, or whatever—you eliminate some of the complexity, narrow the range of the fixings, and make it possible to put your primary emphasis on enjoying the people involved.

Dealing with less food when you entertain means less expense, less preparation, and greater ease of planning. You can take even more of the stress out of the event by inviting others to bring their own favorites of whatever courses you've chosen. Many people enjoy the opportunity to pitch in and even to show off their own skills or choices.

You may want to narrow your food focus even further by making a particular food the theme of your gathering. In season, you might try a late afternoon of everyone's favorite wine and cheese, and create an informal tasting. On a nice weekend, you could host a clambake—

taking responsibility for the shellfish yourself and letting your guests bring along whatever side dishes they want. Arrange a fireside sandwich and movie bash, and let each guest contribute favorite ingredients for a buffet of make-your-own refreshments.

Limiting the food to a single course when you plan a get-together also allows you to limit the duration of the event. An afternoon tea, with simple small sandwiches and pastries, need not last more than a couple of hours. In fact, people expect to leave in time for their own evening plans, knowing that they still have another meal ahead of them.

Sometimes, we fall into patterns of entertaining that are elaborate and time-consuming. When we do, entertaining looms large, and we find ourselves dreading something that is meant to be enjoyable and loving. You need not perpetuate such patterns. Break the trend with a one-course party that brings the enterprise back into the fun zone.

61.

Focus on the Successes of Others

Entertaining—playing host—can completely preoccupy some-one. You get caught up in your plans and preparations. You worry about whether everything will turn out the way that you want and whether your guests will appreciate what you do for them. You focus more than usual on the appearance of your home and your relative ability to make a good event. All in all, if you're not careful, your entertaining becomes all about you.

It pays to take the time to get your head straight as you prepare to extend hospitality of whatever sort. It's true that you are largely responsible for how well planned and executed your event or gathering will be—but *why* are you entertaining? Is it to show off, or is it genuinely to offer a good time to people that you care about?

Plan an event that celebrates someone else's success or good news. Make it your aim to put someone else in the limelight, to give them a great sendoff, or to welcome them into your community. Host a "thank you" party, or take the lead in creating a celebration for the successful conclusion of a community or group effort.

You can also beat the "it's all about me" trap by letting others contribute to what you're planning and then focusing on the parts that they play. If you have a guest who really shines at making some particular food dish, for example, make a point of asking him or her to bring it. Design your own offerings as backdrop or complement, rather than stealing the show with what you make.

Much of the stress that we feel when we entertain has to do with comparisons and the fear of failure. When you learn to focus on the success of others rather than on whether you fail or succeed, you take a big step toward enjoying your own event as a participant instead of as the director. In the process, you give others the pleasure of being honored, praised, and appreciated. Instead of riding the roller coaster of pride, you settle into the warmth and camaraderie of community.

62.

Rearrange the Furniture

There's nothing like the prospect of a party to highlight all of the limitations that you perceive in your home. A smallish room looks even smaller when you imagine a group of people trying to make themselves comfortable in it. An awkward arrangement of public space suddenly becomes the potential setting for tripping feet, falling dishes, or damaged art objects. The lack of multiple bathrooms reminds you that you've never gotten around to decorating the facility at the top of the stairs (certain to be needed by your guests).

Don't let your home's limitations or luxuries stress you out or steal the fun from entertaining. Take a creative look at the space that you've got, and consider what temporary changes you can effect that will make your space more commodious for your guests and less stressful for you.

Begin by depersonalizing the family bathrooms that will need to be available. It takes only moments to put the towels, toothbrushes, bottles, and personal items out of sight. Keep "company" hand towels, a new bar of soap, a candle, and a fresh flower arrangement available to put out an hour before your guests will arrive. With such simple adjustments, you turn your everyday bathrooms into "powder rooms" for your guests.

If you have any breakable objects that could be easily knocked over in a crowd, relocate them for the duration of your party. Some items, as much as you love them, might be better put away than left out to be admired while you hover nearby with your heart in your throat. Likewise, if you have an especially valuable floor covering, consider rolling it up if you're planning a lot of food and drink traffic or dancing. Don't leave a vulnerable surface uncovered if it is a likely repository for glasses or dishes—and make sure that you provide coasters and napkins.

Consider moving furniture so that you provide comfortable groupings for conversation and easy traffic. If you're more interested in showing off the way your house looks undisturbed, invite small enough groups that everyone can move and sit comfortably. If you really want a big group, make the necessary changes to accommodate the number of people you've invited.

Happy entertaining is all about flexibility. Put first things first when you entertain—safety, comfort, and ease. The rest will fall into place without catastrophe.

63.

Let Simplicity Rule

If you find that entertaining consistently plunges you into a stew of anxiety, consider a new approach to the business. Instead of seeking out the most elaborate, complicated, or expensive recipes, decorations, or ideas for your events, apply the simplicity rule. The simplicity rule goes something like this: If you can do with less, do. Think about how you can achieve what you want without turning yourself into a whirling dervish or a nervous wreck.

If you're like most people, when you feel anxious, you tend to complicate your plans and preparations, but far from alleviating your discomfort, your elaborations just make you more stressed than ever. It takes a conscious effort to change that response if it has been your habit over years, but you can change.

When you decide to entertain, begin by considering the basics. Write down your answers to the following questions. Who do you want to invite? What do you want to do with them? Where do you want it to happen? When do you want to do it?

Looking over your answers, think through the consequences of the choices that you've made thus far. Write down any complications that you can foresee in connection with any of your decisions. These would probably relate to having enough time to plan and invite, having the combination of people that you want, or having the resources that you'll need when you need them. Ask yourself: Is there some way that I could adjust this choice to reduce or eliminate the complications I foresee? If your answer is "yes," make the adjustment right now. If your answer is "no," rethink the basics of your plan. You may be setting yourself up for anxiety. You may need to go back to the drawing board.

Once you have the basics decided in a way that creates the least amount of complication, think through each of the decisions that follow with one question always in mind: What will make this simpler for me? If you see the need to eliminate something, do it. If you need to delegate, get on the phone now. If you need to find simpler cooking methods or alternative recipes, give yourself the time to do so.

The specifics to which you apply the simplicity rule will be unique to you and to the particular event that you are planning. If you really put the rule to work, you will find that entertaining becomes an increasingly enjoyable enterprise for you without sacrificing the fun or quality for your guests.

64.

Don't Be Afraid of Bargains

Advertisers have clever ways of suggesting that "only the best" is good enough for company. Anything less, they imply, insults your guests and puts your reputation as a host at risk. Of course, "the best" will almost always translate into the most expensive, and that turns entertaining into a high-cost deal that can blow your budget and raise your stress level.

Don't let the media sell you a bill of goods. Quality does not have to depend on a steep price tag, and bargains do not spell social disaster.

One way to keep the cost of regular entertaining down is to think ahead. If you use standard supplies—candles, cocktail napkins, toothpicks, pantry staples, or beverages—keep an eye out for sales and specials. When you see one of your favorite items marked down, buy a quantity and store it for future occasions. If a store offers a price advantage to buying by the case or in bulk, consider doing so. Make it a habit to watch for the bargains when you're *not* entertaining so that you won't have to add bargain-hunting to your to-do list when an event is at hand.

Another way to make your entertaining affordable is to choose a few more expensive touches to embellish the moderate purchases that supply most of your get-together. Take the time to create or find unusual napkin rings that will make the plainest napkins special. Choose one fancy appetizer, and surround it with such bargains as fresh vegetables, peasant bread, and relishes. Use a few luxury flowers and unusual greens within a bouquet of inexpensive daisies or mums to make it elegant. Take an economical poultry main dish to another level with a rich or earthy complement of wild mushrooms or pâté.

Whether you shop for the big bargains or simply combine bargain elements with a few fancier ones, you can let go of the idea that "only the best" is needed to make a lovely, impressive event. Most of the time, your guests won't know the difference. If your generous efforts to honor your guests—whatever they cost—do go unappreciated by some chance, understand that it's their lack of consideration or good manners, not yours.

65.

Set the Stage

The next time you go into your favorite coffee house or restaurant, take a few minutes to simply absorb the atmosphere. What is it about the place and the way that it is set up that makes it appealing to you? Is it the color scheme? The arrangement of the space? The smells? The lighting? You may never consciously have registered the effect that the setting has on your enjoyment of the place, but you can be sure that it does.

What you do with the space in which you entertain likewise has an effect on both your guests and you. Give some thought and attention ahead of time to what you hope the event will be. Perhaps you have fun and games in mind; or maybe you have a yen for elegance; or maybe you just want your guests to be able to put their feet up, relax, and feel right at home. Whatever your intent, there's a mood to what you plan. Creating an environment that communicates your mood is a simple way to set the stage that you can plan in advance.

Think about lighting. If you intend to play games, people will need bright enough light to read instructions, playing cards, or whatever, so arrange to have a good reading light right where you need it. Candlelight always offers a soft elegance, and an abundance of self-contained, long-burning candles are available for a safer alternative to tapers. They can be placed in great numbers around your space. If you're aiming for relaxed, the indirect light of table lamps makes for a homey feel and a kinder illumination than overhead, ceiling-style lighting does.

Think about themes. If you have something festive in mind, look for low-cost touches that you can use to give a celebratory dash to the scene. Disposable products such as decorator napkins, paper flowers, balloons, crepe paper, and thematic festoons can add a lot. If you're planning an ethnic or regional meal, use food items as decorating elements that go with your theme, and pay attention to colors.

The scene that you set when you entertain is part of the fun, so play with it. It doesn't require a big investment of either time or money. You can do it ahead of time and enjoy the results when the time comes for guests to arrive.

66.

Choose Your Time Thoughtfully

It can be disappointing, to say the least, when you go to a lot of trouble for company only to have them eat and run or excuse themselves on the early side. As host, it's difficult not to take it personally, and insecurities creep in. You begin to wonder if you threw a dud of a party or if your guests came only out of obligation.

You can make such a blow less likely by heading it off at the planning stage. When you make your invitations, take the time to ask potential guests whether the time that you've chosen suits them. People don't always feel free to say, "It's a school night, and we like to be home early for the kids," or "I have an early flight the next morning," or "We'll be coming back from an afternoon event, so we may be a little tired." When you ask, you give them the opening to admit that they have lives outside of your affair that may have an effect.

If you already know some of the time constraints that your guests typically have, take their issues into account. Granted, you're the one hosting the party, and your time issues ought to legitimately be of importance to them, but it's not worth the added stress to knowingly plan an event that your guests will have to stretch to handle.

Keep in mind that unless you communicate that the length of their stay makes a difference to you, your guests have no way of knowing it. Sometimes, simply raising the question of what time works for your guests is enough to signal to them that it matters to you. A little bit of thoughtfulness goes a long way. Your consideration may very well elicit consideration in kind from them. They may even bend their own "rules" a bit out of a desire to honor your gift of hospitality.

One way or another, don't let time become a bugaboo in your entertaining. Be direct and thoughtful in your planning and communicating. You'll avoid unnecessary upset and give your guests a clue about how they can best respond to your efforts on their behalf.

67.

Limit the Duration

People leaving too early can certainly bring a host down, but so can guests overstaying their welcome. Again, the best defense is a good offense. Unless you communicate clearly what your expectations and preferences are, your guests can only guess—and if they have different ideas or druthers from yours, they can easily guess incorrectly.

The most straightforward way to limit the duration of a party is to spell it out at the invitation stage. "We're having a little gathering for appetizers and drinks from five to seven" pretty clearly communicates that you expect people to be on their way in time to catch dinner elsewhere. "We thought that we would have dinner on the early side, since I have a business meeting the following morning" indicates that you want to get to bed on time. "It's supposed to be hot on Saturday, so please come over for a swim; we have plans for later, but they're not until six" is a gentle means of saying that you don't intend to make it an all-day and stay-for-dinner kind of event.

If you need to entertain folks who, as you know from experience, don't take time hints easily, you may want to consider going out and driving separately. Restaurant managers have clever, unobtrusive ways of keeping the turnover going—in other words, they'll handle your time limit for you, because they want to have as many seatings at a given table as they can. By driving separately, you avoid the hanging-on aftermath that can make an evening drag. On the other hand, if everyone is having a perfectly wonderful time, you can always choose to add a spontaneous postscript to your evening with a nightcap at another establishment.

Playing host without a sense that you can control the timing generates a lot of dread in advance and stress on the spot. Eliminate both by taking control from the beginning.

68.

Accept Excuses Gracefully

Inevitably, you will extend many invitations that your intended guests will turn down. For some, this possibility is enough to keep them from offering invitations in the first place. The "no" feels too much like a rejection, and these people prefer to avoid entertaining than to risk that pain.

Don't let the fear of failure or rejection keep you from reaching out to others in hospitality. If you have a will to entertain, do it. Your experience has probably already taught you that you'll receive a much higher percentage of acceptances than you will of people who can't attend. The trick then is to understand "no" without suffering self-doubt or insecurity.

First of all, remember that each and every person you know has an entire universe of commitments, concerns, and habits that have nothing to do with you. Your invitation is one blip on the full screen of most busy people's lives. Statistically speaking, it is impossible that every one of your invitations over the years will be accepted. You might as well recognize this fact and use it to gain perspective when you're tempted to feel hurt.

Keep in mind, as well, that each person has a hidden world, an interior landscape of feelings, which affects the way that he or she responds to the outside world. You may have your feet on the ground about "no" in general, but find the *way* that some people say "no" to be hurtful or aggravating. When a refusal seems curt or tense, never jump to the conclusion that the potential guest's emotional response is to you personally. More often than not, you'll probably discover that this person has something else altogether going on that is slopping over into his or her give and take with you.

Finally, make up your mind to accept "no" with grace when it happens. When you do, you leave the door open for future opportunities with good feelings all around. Most specifically, you feel good about yourself.

69.

Take "No" for an Answer

There's a fine line between communicating your interest in people and being pushy, especially when you really want them to join you for an event. You may be tempted to coax or cajole, thinking that you thereby let them know that they are important to you. Unfortunately, that can easily backfire. Rather than feeling wanted, they may react to the pressure with resistance and discomfort.

Take "no" for an answer. Don't make people explain themselves when they turn you down, and don't engender guilt feelings. It's more than enough to say, "I'm sorry you can't join us. Let's look for another time when we can get together." Responding in such a way communicates both your interest *and* your respect.

In point of fact, no one owes you an explanation for turning you down, although people often offer them. They may feel that politeness requires it. In that case, let the excuses stand, whatever they are. If they sound fishy to you, give people the benefit of the doubt, and be glad that they care enough about your feelings to offer it. If excuses sound mysterious or arouse your curiosity in some way, resist the temptation to ask a lot of questions. To press people on the details potentially lands them in the awkward position of having to talk about what they would prefer to keep to themselves. They may not want to reveal who they're seeing instead of you, what they're *really* doing, or the fact that they don't have plans any more compelling than wanting to stay home.

We all want others to take us at our word, to respect our choices, and give us every benefit of the doubt. Make it a point to treat others the way that you'd like to be treated if you chose to turn an invitation down.

70.

Say "No" with Kindness

The flip side of the guest who turns down your invitation is the guest who not only says "yes," but also wants to change your plan to suit him- or herself. If you have not already been faced with an invitee who wants to change the rules, you will. Forewarned is forearmed. Just as other people have the right to say "no" to your offer, you have the right to say "no" to their special requests.

Consider a common situation: Your guest is a smoker and would like to be able to stay indoors with the company while smoking. Happily, information about the health risks involved in secondhand smoke makes it unnecessary for you to say anything as blunt as, "And smell up *my* house? No way!" You can join the vast majority of individuals in the modern world who simply say, "No, I'd rather you didn't." You can always offer a specific outdoor spot with an ashtray if you want to, communicating that you don't mean to judge or create hardship for your guest. You just want to protect yourself and others from the hazards.

In a less frequent but potentially off-putting situation, a guest has a pet that he or she cannot bear to leave. "You wouldn't mind, would you, if poochie came along? She's a *love!* Wouldn't hurt a soul." There's no reason why you have to introduce someone's pet into the mix if you don't want to, but it would be kinder and wiser to avoid insult. People become highly attached to and emotional about their animals. Without dismissing the person as intrusive, you can either explain that you have a pet of your own that would be highly stressed by the presence of another animal; or that you have never allowed animals in your house and don't want to start. Again, if you have an enclosed porch or other neutral space where the animal could reasonably stay, you might offer that, but you're not under any obligation of good manners to do so. If all else fails, you can always say that you have close friends or relatives with extreme allergies to animals, and you don't want to introduce animal dander or hair into your environment. Only the crassest and most thoughtless person would push against that argument.

People sometimes ask for a change of menu, a change of time, different fellow guests, different levels of fanciness, or the inclusion of their children—the possibilities are as manifold as people are unique. Simply remember that the choice is always yours, and you may sometimes want to say "no." Go ahead and say it. Just say it kindly. The idiosyncrasies of others deserve your respect and sense of humor rather than your animosity.

71.

Know When Hired Help Is a Must

You can derive a high degree of satisfaction from planning and executing your own parties. It's great to look your guests in the eye and say, "I did this." You're likely to receive plenty of kudos, lots of ego-food for "doing it all."

There are times and occasions, however, when the burden of doing all that needs doing far outweighs the praise or personal satisfaction that you might gain. The wise host learns to know the difference between a natural do-it-yourself occasion and an event that requires the kind of help you can only get by hiring it.

When in doubt, figure it out. Count the number of people invited. Consider exactly how much time you'll need to plan, clean, shop, prepare, decorate, serve, and clean up. Think, as well, about the physical energy, supplies, and skills required for what you want. Be ruthless in your figuring. Err on the side of more so that you don't back yourself into a corner with too little time, money, or energy.

Once you have a realistic estimate of what's required, ask yourself if you can—or even *want* to—do everything alone or with only volunteer help. Hiring help does not have to be an all-or-nothing proposition. You can save the jobs that suit you and your time for yourself and hire help for other aspects. You may decide that you want to go all out with an event planner, or you may focus on a caterer alone. You may want to hire help for advance cleaning, serving, and after-party cleanup. Maybe all you need are catered appetizer trays and desserts.

Whatever conclusion you reach, if you have to ask the question about hiring help, chances are that you have a big enough gig that it's a good idea. If you decide that hired help is out of the question for financial reasons, rethink your plans. Pare them down to an event that you really *can* deal with alone. There's no point in throwing an event that breaks the bank or your back. Know when enough is enough, and get help!

72.

Take a Break from Failed Traditions

There's an old saying: "If it's not broken, don't fix it." The point is that you make your life a lot simpler if you keep what works and only fix or replace what doesn't. This is just as true in regard to traditions as it is to cars, computers, or the bathroom plumbing. If you have traditions in your entertaining that continue to work and please everyone involved, there's no great gain in changing them.

Remember, however, that you don't have to treat traditions as though they were set in stone. Sometimes, the tried and true ways of doing things or the usual cast of characters no longer yield the enjoyment or suit the purposes that they once did. Times and circumstances change, and generally speaking, you'll suffer the least stress and enjoy the greatest success by recognizing and accommodating those changes.

Watch for the traditional events that you've come to dread. That's a sure sign that it's time to reevaluate what you're doing and how. Pay attention, as well, to a growing sense of boredom or indifference to traditions that used to generate energy and enthusiasm. Take note of the times when this kind of entertaining sparks resentment or anger in you. Any level of chronic negativity associated with a tradition should be your clue that it's time for a change.

Many traditions in entertaining relate to family events. Altering family traditions can raise some prickly feelings, in part because you're dealing with many viewpoints and preferences while also wading into some relatively emotional territory. If you typically host a family event that has become a burden in some way, don't just swallow your feelings. Organize a family powwow to discuss your issues and explore positive ways in which your complaints can be handled.

With friends, as well, the direct approach—as long as you practice a little tact—is almost always the best. You may choose to simply suggest new ways to handle a traditional event, which will imply that you need a change, or you may choose to explain your needs and look to your friends to help come up with the solutions.

In any case, no matter what the tradition, pay attention to the effects of time and change. By all means, if all is well, relax and enjoy. On the other hand, if it's broken, go ahead and fix it. If it can't be fixed, eliminate it and start a new tradition.

73.

Experiment in Advance

S ome ideas are too complicated and elaborate for everyday use. New equipment, fancy meals, special dishes, extraordinary decorations, or unusual combinations of food, drink, activity, and setting beg for an audience. For the adventurous, entertaining others offers an ideal occasion not only for the extra effort but also for experiments.

Before you get too carried away experimenting on company, however, count the cost. You can be sure that your stress level will rise with every element of suspense you introduce into your entertaining. If you have never tried something before, you can't know how it will turn out or whether it will please and satisfy your guests. Since one of the purposes of inviting guests is to offer them a special treat, delving into the unknown raises the success stakes quite a bit.

Experimenting allows for creativity and excitement, so by all means, go for it. Just keep the stress level down by testing your ideas in advance. Make sure that you know what you're doing and what results you're capable of achieving. Go in search of ingredients or supplies well ahead of time. Try testing batches of new recipes without the pressure of guests. Acquaint yourself with a new appliance, whether it's a gas grill, a stovetop smoker, a camera, or a DVD player, and assure yourself that you can operate it without undue fiddling or frustration.

Necessity or inspiration may encourage you to try a small experiment at the last minute. That's fine. On the whole, however, if you want to entertain with confidence and success, do your experimenting before an event so you have as little of the unknown in the mix as possible.

74.

Take the Advice of Experts

Maybe you're one of those people who love to figure out everything on their own. You get a kick out of calculating how much food and drink you'll need for a party of fifty people. You thrive on the excitement of trying a gourmet method of cooking for the first time—without instruction. You have bright ideas about how to illuminate an acre of lawn for a nighttime event.

Good for you, if you enjoy a challenge. Just remember that living in the information age has some great advantages that can make your life easier and your entertaining experiences more foolproof. Information on just about anything that you care to know is readily available on the Internet, through library sources, and out of the mouths of various "experts." You don't have to go it alone.

If you're trying something new, allow yourself the time to get all the facts straight about how to do it *before* you're under time pressure. Go online and search for the answers to any questions that you have. Call the service providers who are relevant to adventures in outdoor lighting (you can overload a circuit before you know it), adequate facilities, makeshift spaces such as tents and dance floors, and other unusual accessories.

Asking for expert advice not only helps to assure a successful outcome, it serves safety concerns. There are right ways and wrong ways to do almost everything. In some cases, the stakes are not high. Disaster simply means that dinner doesn't look or taste the way you wanted—disappointing but not life-threatening. In other cases, however, failure to know the facts may actually put your guests and you at risk. The cautionary information on gadgets, the safe-handling instructions for perishable foods, and the general safety rules promoted by such organizations as fire departments and the American Red Cross appear for good reason. They have been developed because serious accidents can and do happen when you least expect them. Education is your best defense.

Let the experts have their say. Know what you're doing when you entertain so that you can provide the most enjoyable and safest time possible for everyone involved.

75.

Make People the Main Attraction

Food, activities, decorations, and ambience all contribute to entertaining that is well-planned and successful. It's possible, though, to get so caught up in your plans and preparations that you neglect the most important element of entertaining—your guests.

No matter how elaborate you choose to make your event, you can still focus on the people you invite as the main attraction. What does this mean? In the first place, it means that you maintain a balance between the "stuff" of the party and the people. Any time that material concerns take precedence over human issues—you're annoyed that you have to rearrange the entire table setting to accommodate John's left-handedness or Melanie's leg cast, for instance—you can be sure that you've lost your people perspective. Whenever you feel your own barometer swinging toward the negative, check your priorities. If your guests have slipped out of center position, adjust your focus.

Keeping people at the center also means that you redirect attention away from yourself and your efforts and toward your guests.

Everyone appreciates recognition, but you can allow a little of it to go a long way. When you are praised, thank your admirers with grace, and then take the initiative to change the course of the conversation. Encourage topics that take you out of the spotlight and draw others into the give and take.

Finally, plan and prepare with an eye to making yourself available to your guests when you entertain. When you let other concerns take first importance—fussing over last-minute food preparation, answering the telephone, playing with the CD selection, or whatever—you put your guests on notice that they do not have your full attention. By extension, that communicates that they are of less importance to you than a million other details.

Life offers each of us nothing more precious than our relationships with others. Don't let the details of entertaining overshadow that fact. Your guests—the people in your life—want *you* far more than they want what you *do*. Focus on the people. The rest will follow.

76.

Establish the Mood

When you entertain, you have the opportunity to set the stage and orchestrate the elements of your event to suit you. Beyond choosing and preparing the food and activities, it's up to you to decide what mood you want to strike. Do you want to go for elegance or a casual feel? Do you prefer a lot of noise and fun for the occasion, or peace and relaxation? Are you aiming at intimate or formal?

Remember that it's hard to score a bull's-eye when you don't know what your target is. Think ahead about the mood you want for your guests. Then consider how you can promote that mood with each choice that you make. Alert your guests when you invite them in regard to dress style so they can anticipate the mood before they ever arrive. Greet them at the door with a welcome that suits the ambience, and carry the flavor of the occasion into food, drink, music, lighting, setting, activity, and pace.

You are just as influential as the trappings of your entertaining when it comes to setting the mood. Your manner leads the way for the people you've invited. If you behave in a formal manner, they will almost certainly follow your lead. If you are jolly, they will relax into a lighthearted mode. If you set a serious tone, your guests will settle down for a sober time.

Perhaps the most important aspect of the ambience that you establish will be the degree to which you make your guests feel wanted and welcome. You demonstrate this by the warmth of your greeting, the way that you notice and honor needs, and the words that you offer. A simple toast that thanks your guests for their presence communicates your appreciation and pleasure. In this, too, you can lead the way. As your guests feel your warmth, they will more often than not respond in kind.

77.

Lighten the Mood

There's the mood that you set, and then there's the mood that develops in any gathering of individuals. People arrive at an event with their own dispositions, driven by a combination of temperament, occurrences of their day, worries, joys, and sorrows of their own. They will pick up the mood that you've set for the occasion, but they'll also affect it. The more people who are involved, the greater the number of psychological exchanges that can change the tenor of the gathering.

You are not a victim of your guests' behavior unless you allow yourself to be. When the tone of an occasion goes south, it's up to you to smooth over the moment and bring it back to what you want it to be. If there's friction between guests, you're the one who needs to step in to redirect the conversation toward safer subjects. If someone falls into a funk, it's you who should draw them into the conversation of others to lead them away from their own dark thoughts. If things get a little too raucous, you can quiet them down with an announcement of the next course of food, a change of location from one room to another, or a piece of music that "you really want them to hear."

Hosting involves an equal measure of planning and attention, with a little bit of magic thrown in. You need to be in the thick of the company that you assemble, because you are the maestro of your own event. As you observe and relate to your guests, you subtly keep the party on track with small interventions and redirections. Don't give up your leadership role. Take responsibility for the mood as it develops. If things get out of hand for a while, don't fret. Just assert your position as host. In most cases, your guests will respect that role and respond accordingly.

78.

Offer "Rain Dates"

Even the best-laid entertaining plans can go awry. The weather turns treacherous, people become ill, world events intervene, or traffic comes to an irreversible standstill. As host, you have the option of proceeding as planned, no matter what—or you can take the pressure off everyone involved by offering to reschedule. In some cases, all that's needed is a slightly later start as you wait for people to make their adjustments for the unexpected.

However, there are times when an event simply cannot go forward. This is when flexibility needs to rule. While calling off a sumptuous meal at the last minute feels disappointing to the person who prepared it, it is not the end of the world. Watching all of your outdoor decorations wilt and sag under a drenching rain may bring you down and cost you some pennies, but it doesn't cause human damage. It's only stuff. Stuff comes and goes at the best of times. What matters is people.

When disasters and acts of God subvert your plans, take it easy and regroup. Ask yourself what is best for your guests. Put yourself in their shoes, and honor their concerns and interests. Be ready and willing to say, "It sounds as though today isn't going to work out the way that we hoped. Please don't worry about it. Let's concentrate on rescheduling."

In the meantime, you may find that you can create something spontaneous and enjoyable even out of disaster. Are your guests snowed out of a great feast that's ready and waiting for people who now can't come? How about inviting your snowbound neighbors over to share in the bounty? Do you have a wonderful supply of appetizers and desserts? Divide the goods up in quantities that would suit drop-in visits and spur-of-the-moment invitations. Then label and freeze them. You'll be a party waiting to happen the next time someone comes by.

The key here is simple. Things happen. Plans have to be changed. The more you fret and fuss, the bigger you make the problem, and the more awkward your almost-guests feel. If you learn to roll with the wind, adjust your sails, and choose a new course, you can go beyond limiting the damages to actually making something new and fun out of a disappointment.

79.

Mind Your Manners

Everyone loves a good, old-fashioned party. In fact, sometimes people love a good time a little too much. When the company relaxes into a raucous, anything-goes mode, the results can range from funny to tedious to dangerous, especially if alcohol consumption is involved. Even if it's not what you as host intend or expect, you may find yourself with an individual or group who has gotten out of hand.

Even if you enjoy a wild time as much as the next person, you bear real responsibilities as host. When a gathering begins to get rowdy or sloppy, you are the one who needs to take it in hand and calm things down. You may have to act as arbiter, bartender, or bouncer. You may need to confiscate car keys, put alcohol away, and bring out the water and coffee, or find a place for someone to lie down. First and foremost, you need to be aware and awake.

In the midst of fun and games, when people are letting their hair down, make it your job to maintain the basic boundaries of common sense and thoughtful conduct. You'll save yourself and your guests embarrassment, hurt feelings, or worse.

80.

Steer Away from Gossip

Gossip is one of the most destructive forces that exists in community life. The fact that it is all around us all of the time does not take away from its power to skew the truth and hurt both feelings and reputations. At some level, most of us know this, yet the temptation to talk about others is so great that we often indulge, regardless.

When you gather people together for a social event, you provide the perfect setting for gossip. Your guests inevitably know people in common whom you did not invite or who could not attend, and a juicy bit of information about such an absentee can quickly get the tongues wagging. The next thing you know, you have a veritable gabfest of speculations, opinions, judgments, and misinformation about someone who, by his or her absence, is rendered helpless to defend him- or herself.

As host, you can set a different tone. You don't have to let gossip reign. Change the subject, redirect attention, pull the focus away from the absent to those who are present, put on some dance tunes—in other words, do whatever you need to do to transform the flow of conversation. If all else fails, simply say, "Max is my friend. I really don't feel comfortable talking about him when he's not here," or, "I don't know Diane very well, but I'm sure that she wouldn't like to think we're talking about her here."

Many people disguise gossip in the language of concern, or they pretend to be discussing something about the missing person with that person's well-being at heart. They begin their comments about someone who isn't in the mix with a caveat like, "Don't misunderstand me. I love Pat to pieces, but…" Don't be fooled. Gossip by any other name is still gossip, and it still does harm. You don't want to gain the reputation as the host whose parties are dangerous to miss.

The bottom line is this: No one likes to be discussed behind his or her back. In gossip, as in so much of life, the Golden Rule should be applied. Treat others the way you'd like them to treat you.

81.

Set the Table Ahead of Time

You can entertain in a big way or stick to small affairs, but in either case, you end up with a list of jobs that you need to accomplish in preparation. The jobs, like the events themselves, come in all sizes, from the big task of making a special meal or decorating an acre of lawn to the little chores that no one will notice but that you still have to do.

You may be inclined to let go of the mindless details in deference to the major work in preparation for your event. In some situations, that may be the right choice for effective time management. Just remember that all of those small jobs add up to a significant amount of time and labor, too. If you leave them all until the last minute, you may find yourself zooming around, running out of time, and building up a case of the sweats just when you want to be calm and collected to greet your guests.

Go ahead and give first priority to the larger, more complicated preparations. Knowing that you've adequately planned and prepared the featured events will go a long way toward relieving your mind and keeping everything under control. While you're at it, though, take advantage of a moment here and a moment there to tackle some of the smaller preparations. If you're serving a meal in a formal dining room that you don't use every day, set the table a day in advance. Lay out your serving area with utensils and hot plates. Buy fresh candles and put them in their holders throughout the entertaining space. Polish the glass on the front of the hutch. Gather the fresh herbs that you want and place them in a vase of water for easy, last-minute access.

If a small-scale job can be completed in a matter of five or ten minutes, it's worthy of being done ahead of time, in a few spare moments. The advantage of crossing such jobs off the list in advance is obvious. The psychological advantage, while less plain to see, is just as significant. There's nothing quite as satisfying as finishing a job. The little things can be completed and crossed off in a wink. Give yourself the head start and the psychic lift of completing small tasks.

82.

Go Ethnic

In an age when the globe has shrunk to the size of a newspaper page or a television screen, we have a constant flow of ethnic images before us from around the world. Because the geopolitical realities are generally tense, these glimpses can often be alarming. Yet what we witness also exists in a much larger context of real people just like you, but with their own unique cultures of lifestyles, beliefs, customs, and culinary habits. The abundance of information available to everyone through the media and the Internet means that if we want to know more about a particular place, we can.

Stuck for a party plan? In search of a good theme? Why not focus some of your entertaining on a particular ethnic culture? Choose a place in the news and gather information on the diet and customs of the people there. Gather recipes, and select those that can be done with ingredients available where you live. Look for pictures of the decorations and attire used for more formal occasions or for festivals and celebrations, and let them guide you in decorating for your event.

If you're lucky enough to have some diversity among your friends and acquaintances, consider making a round robin of events that feature the various represented cultures. The person whose ethnicity is the focus can serve as "consultant" for the elements involved. You could also throw a party in which all of the cultures represented in the group have a place on the menu, in the activities, or in the décor—a smorgasbord of identities.

An ethnic theme can be carried to extremes or kept low-key, depending on your resources, enthusiasm, and desires. In any case, it gives you a peg on which to hang your entertaining hat. Much more than that, it allows you to explore the world of another set of people, to step inside their shoes in a small way and understand who they are. It may offer only a tiny glimpse for a very short duration, but if it adds even a dash of sympathy and fellow feeling to our world, it's worth it.

83.

Choose Your Battles

Any entertaining you do—whether it's an intimate dinner party or a big bash—calls for work on your part and negotiations with all of the participants. You may know exactly what you want to do, but when you issue your invitations, you may discover that one aspect of it or another needs to be revisited. It's in the revisiting—the shifts and finagling needed to make an event happen—that you may find your stress level rising.

You'll be at your best to handle such stress if you keep a clear picture in your mind of what you want to accomplish. Consider why you're entertaining in this particular situation. Think carefully about all of the various aspects of the plans you've made. Figure out what about the event means the most to you—what you feel strongly about. You can't respond reasonably or exercise flexibility without knowing what is bendable and what is not.

When you face challenges to your plans, consider them in relation to the priority list built on your considerations. You can stand fast on exactly the guest list you want, the time you've chosen, the sorts of activities or food you've planned, and other such details—or you can make compromises that allow you to go forward with some version of your plans while still accommodating the needs, requests, or conflicts of others. In the first case, you face frustration at best, and very possibly a total cancellation of your event at worst. In the second, your entertaining is still a go, but with alterations that take others into account.

Life is full of challenges. The key to facing them with some level of equanimity is the ability to choose your battles. Some things are worth standing firm on. These have to do with taking care of your soul—accomplishing what really matters and guarding yourself from situations that put too much strain on you. However, you can afford to be flexible about other things. These have more to do with standing on ceremony—issues of pride and stubbornness—than they do with real concerns. Know the difference, and choose your battles accordingly. You'll come out of your entertaining with far fewer scars as a result.

84.

Avoid Last-Minute Fuss

You can plan the most stupendous event in the world, with all the bells and whistles, no holds barred, but if you want your guests to have a great time, you need to make sure that the host is in good condition when they arrive. Your hosting depends on your state of mind more than anything else. This means that you need to be calm, collected, and capable of having a good time yourself. Nothing subverts this faster than last-minute fuss that works you up into a lather.

You don't have to fall victim to last-minute fuss. With a combination of sound planning and a reasonable perspective, you can rise above whatever confronts you in the final minutes before your guests arrive.

First, plan for the many last-minute details well in advance. Take the time to think through all that you want done. Walk through the event in your mind, and record every detail that occurs to you. Then make sure you're whittling away at the to-do list as you have time, so that everything doesn't fall in your lap at the last minute.

Second, be prepared to let go of anything that doesn't really matter if time runs short. Fold the napkins conventionally instead of the fancy way you intended. Forget about having all of the music queued for the evening. You can take a moment here or there once your guests arrive to change CDs or pull more music out of the rack. Let guests help you assemble appetizer trays instead of having them entirely ready and waiting. Putting yourself in a frenzy over these activities will only take away from your ability to be a thoughtful host.

Finally, concentrate on having *you* ready. Of all the elements that combine to make your entertaining a success, *you* are by far the most important. If you're relaxed, happy to greet your guests, and at ease with whatever state they find you in, they'll be fine. If you're frazzled and upset, scurrying around with sweat on your brow and anxiety written all over your face, your guests will be tense and uncomfortable. Plan to be dressed and groomed in plenty of time. (You can always use an apron if you're concerned about keeping your clothes clean.) Give yourself leeway for early arrivals—and keep reminding yourself that your guests are what matter most to you.

85.

Make Available What You Need

Even in a time when we enjoy an abundance of almost anything that we can put our imaginations to, we can sometimes have trouble laying hands on exactly the item we want. Especially if you strive for something unusual, you may discover that certain ingredients or objects are not readily available. They're out of stock, sold only in specialty stores, or obtainable only by catalog. As always, your best defense against being caught short of a vital item is advance planning.

Before you build too much on an unusual or complicated plan, make a complete list of what you need. Then locate each item, one by one, and assure yourself that it will be available when you need it. You may need to place a special order for your specific time frame, or you may discover that you have to do without something. By starting ahead of time with acquiring what you need, you'll allow yourself time to research substitutes and obtain them instead.

Some things—rented tents, linens, tables, and perishable food, beverage, or flower items—have to wait. Once you've made arrangements for these types of items, note on your calendar to confirm your orders several days in advance of when you'll pick them up or have them delivered. This is standard operating procedure for anyone in the event-planning business. Professionals know that even prepaid orders can sometimes go awry due to late returns by others, mistakes in paperwork, or late shipments. You want to know if your order has gone astray with enough time to make alternative plans.

Most of all, never build your entertaining around assumptions that you can get what you need when you need it. It doesn't require a great deal of effort to check ahead—but it saves an enormous amount of aggravation and panic.

86.

Invite Your Guests to Begin

Some folks find it more difficult than others to get everything to the table before guests take their seats for a meal. Even the more efficient hosts often find that last-minute surveys of the table or requests from guests keep them running back to the kitchen while the food sits untouched in the serving platters.

Don't let your late kitchen runs get in the way of serving your guests hot food in a timely manner. It's entirely within the rules of good manners to invite your guests to begin to serve themselves before you sit. Simply say, "Please, go ahead and serve yourselves." If people seem slow or reluctant, pause long enough to pass a serving plate to someone and tell others specifically what you would like them to start on.

Likewise, even after you and everyone else have your plates full and are ready to eat, you may discover that you've left the bread in the oven, neglected to put butter on the table, or missed filling someone's water glass. Whatever the issue, you need to hop up from the table one more time. Take the time to raise a toast to your guests or wish them "Bon appétit," take your own first bite, encourage others to do the same, and then make your kitchen run. Under such conditions, people will feel comfortable getting started without you at the table.

As you work your way through several courses, you may find that your serving duties keep you busy and away from the table. The same rules apply throughout the meal. You don't have to be at the table for good manners' sake, but you need to let people know that you'll only be a minute and really want them to begin. Then make sure that you really *are* only a minute. You'll blend right into the conversation and festivities, and your guests will get to eat while the food is in mint condition.

87.

Don't Wait for Over-Late Guests

Even with the best will and the most scrupulous planning, you can't control what your guests do. Although many people understand that honoring the specific time of a meal invitation, within twenty minutes at the outside, is mandatory for courtesy's sake, you'll likely run into someone in the course of entertaining who has a real problem with punctuality.

You don't have to let someone else's time troubles spoil an event for you and the rest of your guests. Sometimes, things happen that are beyond the control of your guests. They hit traffic, suffer their own car troubles, or have last-minute emergencies. They owe it to you, in such situations, to call and alert you to the fact that they'll be late. If they'll arrive within reasonable proximity of the time that you planned to actually sit down to the meal, you may want to postpone everyone's eating to allow them to start with the rest. If they'll obviously be too late for the good of the food, it's okay to say, "Get here when you can. Don't worry. We'll get started on time and you can catch up."

What about people who just can't pull it together to make a timely appearance, for whatever reason? They may call, they may not, but they push beyond the invited time of arrival by an hour or more. The first time it happens, you may hold the meal in good faith that they will arrive at any moment. At the point at which you know that the food will be spoiled, go ahead and serve everyone else. Don't make everyone suffer because of one or two people's rudeness. Let the time problem of the latecomers be theirs alone.

Once burned by latecomers, learn your lesson. If you're willing to invite them to a meal another time, make it clear at the outset that you won't hold dinner for their lateness. Tell them when you hope that people will arrive. Tell them, as well, exactly when you intend to have the meal on the table. That way, you'll make clear that the time is set. If they arrive to a meal already in progress, they have only themselves to blame.

88.

Mix Up the Seating

Hosts often choose to mix up their guests for the sake of interesting conversation when seating them at a table. Some aim to mix genders, making sure that the seating falls roughly male-female all the way around. Others aim to separate spouses, with the idea that couples can speak to one another at any time, and this is their chance to have some give and take with other people. Still others try to put people together who have common interests, similar backgrounds, or other tie-ins that will give them good fodder for talk and amusement. In all of these situations, a host hopes to make the party lively and keep the guests stimulated.

If you have a regular group of people who get together often, you may find mixed seating valuable for other reasons, as well. Some combinations of people prove to be less than helpful to the success of a gathering. For example, a pair of people who have an unusually tight relationship as friends and have a lot to talk about in low, confidential voices can make others feel like outsiders. You may find it advantageous to encourage such a pair to go their own ways for the duration of your event.

Alternatively, you may be aware of conflict between certain people—for example, people who once dated or were married but have since separated. To place them next to one another may be just enough to make their tensions spill over to your other guests. No one wants to fall victim to the bad feelings of others. You can spare your company that discomfort by either not inviting warring or alienated factions to the same event or making sure that they don't have to sit shoulder to shoulder.

Whether you mix it up to make for more fun, control cliquishness, or limit tension, you relieve your own stress and do your guests a favor. Just make sure that you exercise some tact and sensitivity. It may be helpful to double-check your seating plan with someone else who knows the people involved. "I thought I'd put so-and-so there, and who's-it here. Does that sound good to you?" Your care in placing people can add comfort and pleasure to the gathering.

89.

Plan a Final Heads-Up

Thanks to the treadmill of modern living, folks often fall into the trap of filling their time to the limit. One obligation is piled atop another, and daily business is planned out in segments roughly approximating the schedule in a TV guide.

When you plan to entertain, you may use the same sort of scheduling to complete everything that you need to do. If so, you're adding stress and strain to entertaining that you could eliminate.

First, make up your mind that you're going to keep time on a more leisurely schedule. Give yourself some leeway when you work out the timing for entertaining. Don't give yourself just enough time to squeak in under the wire of the first guest's arrival. Try aiming for complete readiness with a half-hour or more to spare. In the time remaining, you can look over your preparations to double-check their condition. You can run down your menu or plan and make sure that you've remembered everything. You can check the lavatory one last time for guest-readiness. Additionally, you can start the music to put yourself in the entertaining frame of mind.

With time to spare, you can actually allow yourself to sit down, put your feet up, and catch your breath. More often than not, people arrive at their own parties and events in a state of rush and tension. They sometimes don't begin to enjoy themselves until the gig is almost finished, because they've pushed so hard to get there in the first place. With a little rest and reflection time, you can offer your guests the smiling face and relaxed demeanor of someone ready to have a good time. In the process, you give yourself the gift of being fully present and prepared, and stress goes out the window.

90.

Practice Composure

The dictionary defines "composure" as "calmness or repose of mind, or self-possession." These are descriptions of an attitude, something that happens first in your thinking, and then by extension, in your feelings and actions. The quality of composure allows you to receive the challenges of everyday life without going to pieces or carrying an excess of stress. That makes it especially valuable when you entertain, an activity that carries its share of challenges.

Although people exist who arrived on this planet with a natural gift for composure, most have to work for it, because it does not come naturally to them. Happily, you can learn to assume a composed state of mind, and with practice, you can maintain it when the stress builds.

Practicing composure is referred to by some as the "relaxation response." The practice involves both recognition of your stressed state and a proactive response to that state. It requires consciousness and a willingness to apply new solutions to old habits.

Try this when you have a free ten- or fifteen-minute period of time. First, find a comfortable, quiet place to sit. Assume a sitting position that you can maintain at ease for the full time. Beginning at your toes and working your way to the top of your head, notice how tense or relaxed each of your muscle groups is and consciously let go of any tension that you discover. When you've reached a still, relaxed posture, you're ready to move on.

Now, close your eyes and picture a place that you find pleasant. Imagine that you are sitting or walking there right now. Take in the light, colors, smells, and sounds. As you imagine, take a deep, slow breath, filling your lungs completely from bottom to top. Hold the air for a moment, and then slowly breathe it out until your lungs are as empty as you can make them. Repeat this breathing technique for a minimum of ten minutes. You can keep time with a timer so that you aren't distracted by watching the clock.

This relaxation exercise, practiced regularly, teaches you how to put yourself in a composed state, helps you to learn how to recognize the tension that you carry, and gives you experience in composure. In other words, you learn to know the difference between tension and composure. Over time, with practice, you will be able to return to that composed state without actually going through the entire exercise.

91.

Lead with Your Heart

Entertaining is just one of many, many ways which we relate to one another in life. We do it to spend time with our friends, to express our interest or thanks to acquaintances, to share our bounty with our community, or to bring our families together. It's about extending hospitality and offering a bit of ourselves to others.

However, the details can sometimes overwhelm us. In all of the fuss and activity of planning, preparing, and making a social event happen, we can lose sight of the reason that we entertain. The event itself takes on a life and personality of its own, and the people and relationships that motivated it recede into the background. When our plans and desires become more important than the people who are involved, our attitudes run amok, and stress builds.

Don't let your plans overtake you. Keep your focus firmly on people, whether they are your guests or other people who will be affected by your plans—your kids, spouse, neighbors, or people that you chose not to invite. Think with pleasure about giving your guests an enjoyable experience. Consider with compassion how to be thoughtful about the noise that you'll make, the cars that will take up parking space, and the time that people are giving up to be there or to help. Handle with generosity and gratitude the help that you may receive or hire. In other words, lead with your heart.

Life takes its toll on all of us. There's not a person alive who doesn't need and appreciate a little tender loving care. When you entertain, you welcome people to enjoy some of your tender loving care. You can alleviate a lot of your own stress and bother by making that attitude your guide as you entertain.

92.

Include Make-Aheads

A party that includes food and drink can pose a juggling challenge at just the time that the guests start to arrive. Inevitably, a meal involves some last-minute work. The meat needs to be carved, the canapés need heating and serving, drinks need to be poured, hot vegetables must be cooked. All in all, the kitchen can sometimes turn into a three-ring circus that leaves little or no time for greeting, circulating among guests, or composing yourself.

You can take some of the strain off by not only planning but also making ahead. Many wonderful dishes exist that can be entirely prepared ahead of time. In fact, it's possible to create a whole event that uses nothing but foods that are made and arranged in advance.

Whether you choose to have a low-maintenance meal such as a sandwich and dessert buffet that requires no last-minute cooking, or offer up a full-course formal dinner with a variety of dishes that all need to reach the table hot, take advantage of make-ahead options. Choose your menu with at least a good balance of foods that you make ahead of time and last-minute foods so that your work is cut by at least half. If you plan raw or precooked items, do some of the presentation ahead of time so that you only have to remove the plastic wrap or foil when the time comes. If you have dishes that can be partly prepared ahead, use that option to give yourself the maximum leeway at party time.

Think, too, about assembling premeasured and prechopped ingredients for a dish that demands on-the-spot cooking. Imagine yourself as a television chef with all that you need ready and waiting around you.

Just about any meal has room for plenty of advance cooking and preparing. The more you take advantage of that, the more relaxed you'll be when it's time to put the meal into action. The more relaxed you are, the more fun you and your guests will have.

93.

Consider Collaborating

In general, hosting tends to be performed as a solo or duet in the same household. The people offering their home or their efforts take primary responsibility, however much they delegate or share the load of details in an event. The stress of making it happen and succeed falls squarely and solely on their shoulders.

There's more than one way to make hosting less of a burden and—with luck and good planning—a lot more fun. The next time that you plan to gather a group of your favorite people, consider joining forces with a friend to be co-hosts.

Co-hosts take equal responsibility for the work, the pleasure, the blame, and the credit. They put their heads together for every step involved in the event, from planning and inviting to preparing, welcoming, and serving to the last details of cleaning up. If one of the co-hosts provides the place, the other may take full charge of the invitations. If one chooses the music, the other may decide on decorations—and so on and so forth.

Co-hosting allows you accomplish the usual event with half the work—or it allows you to throw a party twice the size of what you'd usually do with only the work that a smaller event would require. It gives you the great benefit of another pair of hands, feet, and eyes, and an alternative set of ideas.

Maybe best of all is the fun that you can have getting ready for a party. When you are solely in charge, the tension can mount in a hurry. You know that it's all up to you. When you share the hosting with someone else, you have company in all that you do. You can rest in the knowledge that someone else is also paying attention to the many details, and you can enjoy the process.

94.

Beware the Spoilers

You get to know people and their peculiarities at close range when you spend social time with them. With some people, you're in for delightful surprises regarding their interests and qualities, and knowing them a little better whets your appetite to know them all the more. There are those, however, whose peculiarities make poor mixing material for a social occasion. Not only do they exhibit behavior that you could happily do without, but they create an atmosphere that detracts from the pleasure of the time for everyone around them. A few hours with them turn out to be more than enough.

Such spoilers come in a number of flavors. They may be loudmouths who cannot share the stage, bigots whose opinions offend, drunks who become sloppy or obnoxious, or scrappers who turn every conversation into a fight. Whatever their brand of boorishness, spoilers can turn an otherwise lovely time into a chore that other guests rush to escape.

If you feel social pressure to invite a particular problem person when you entertain, you need not cave in to it. One of the great bonuses to hosting is the power to choose your company. The first time that a guest you've invited shows him- or herself to be a spoiler, you can chalk it up as their problem. The second time you invite them, you have no one to blame but yourself.

If one half of a couple is the problem, make it a point to do most of your socializing one on one (or in events staged for "girls" or "boys" only) with the spouse that you like. You can also entertain the couple without others involved and in ways that allow you to control how much time you have to spend with them. For example, meeting for a light restaurant meal gives you a good measure of flexibility.

Even if your spoiler happens to be a family member, you can limit the time you spend with the person. Keep the big, obligatory family gatherings to a minimum. Find ways other than home entertaining to maintain your ties to the loved ones attached to the problem person. You may even find that some direct talk with other family members is needed to control the potential damage of the family spoiler.

You can be victimized by the bad behavior of another person only if you allow it. Don't allow it. Life is short, and relationships are plentiful. Spend your entertaining time and effort on the people that you enjoy and appreciate. Let the others go.

95.

Develop Specialties

A social event that you host can give you the opportunity to try new, fancy, or unusual dishes. An expanded audience makes the added time and effort that you spend in preparation seem worth it. Yet there are times when company is coming that you have more desire than time to prepare something wonderful and novel.

That's when there's nothing quite like your old, oft-repeated recipes for ease and speed. Familiarity gives them the advantage of the known—you know what you are doing, and you know how the food will turn out. The combination of comfort level and predictability relieves the pressure created by time constraints.

However, the tried and true may or may not strike you as company-worthy food. You feel caught, and the idea of entertaining loses its zip. You don't have to stick to what you've done in the past. It's never too late to develop new old favorites that you can whip out when you want to entertain but time is short. This calls for some advance thought, obviously. *Before* you need it, when you find a recipe that you enjoy making, get to know it, fiddle with it until you're happy with it, and turn it into a specialty. Present it well, and encourage people to think of it as "yours." Better yet, get to know the dish so well that it *feels* like yours.

Aside from the obvious advantage of serving surefire winners time and again, personal specialties in your culinary repertoire make it easier to be prepared for short notice. Make sure that you have the essential ingredients in the freezer and pantry, if possible, so that you can create a favorite at the last minute. Choose recipes that store well in the freezer, and make double batches when you plan to serve them, freezing half for a spontaneous dinner party at another time.

Whatever the event, it always pays to have some specialties that you can pull out of your recipe box in a pinch. Your guests won't be disappointed to see a repeat of a former success. In fact, you may find friends and family requesting your special dishes.

96.

Use an Icebreaker as Your Theme

Holidays, celebrations, and traditional family occasions often serve as organizing elements for entertaining. When your guests don't know one another well, however, you may want to focus your entertaining on a theme specifically designed to break the ice and help people become better acquainted.

For example, one host may use name cards and a pen at each table setting, then ask each guest to write an unusual fact about him- or herself on the back. The host can then collect the cards, read out the facts one at a time, and let guests guess whom each fact describes. Such a device is simple, but it can lead both to stimulating conversation and a growing interest among the individuals involved.

Your choice of icebreaker is limited only by your imagination. It doesn't need to take much time or preparation. It only needs, as the term suggests, to warm up the interaction a bit. Your goal is to get folks talking, especially when you have a group of people who don't know one another well. You can take some of the suspense and tension out of the scene by giving them a way to get started.

97.

Let Go of Expectations

When you entertain, it's unavoidable that you invest yourself in the outcome. You've put time and effort into creating an occasion, and you want it to be a success. If the event doesn't turn out as you hoped or expected, you feel disappointed and deflated. The next time that you entertain, you go into it with a little less confidence and a tad more anxiety. Your fears actually begin to erode the qualities that make you a good host, which increases the possibility that the outcome will not measure up to your hopes.

This sort of spiraling emotional track gathers momentum over time if you allow it to do so. That's why the best cure is to nip it in the bud, and you're the only one who can wield the pruning shears. You need to recognize what is going on in your head and redirect your thinking. This may sound like a Herculean task when you're in the midst of stressing over a coming event, but all that it actually takes is some conscious reflection on life as it really is.

Understand, first of all, that entertaining, like all human interaction, is essentially organic. There's a limit to what you can pre-program, because people are full of quirks and surprises. If you go into an event with a set idea of what an occasion must be for you to feel that it is successful, you stand a good chance of suffering disappointment—not because the occasion failed, but because you limited your definition of success too narrowly.

Keep in mind, as well, that other people have their own ideas of what constitutes a great time. Don't even bother trying to read other people's minds on the subject. You can't predict the reactions of others. Make your plans according to what suits you, doing your best to take your guests into consideration without turning it into a worry.

Bottom line: What will be will be. You may see your fondest hopes realized or host an event that bears little or no resemblance to what you imagined. With the right mindset, you can enjoy either eventuality. Let go of expectations and go with the flow. Planning is only planning. Life, with all its vagaries, is the adventure.

98.

Keep Your Intention in Mind

The hubbub and logistics of entertaining can easily eat up your energy and focus if you let them. In the midst of all of your preparation and hosting, your fundamental reason for throwing an event—whether it's a simple dinner party or a grand reception—can be lost in the shuffle. When that happens, you open the door to emotional responses that detract from your enjoyment and coping ability.

Offset the possibility of losing yourself in the busywork of entertaining by adjusting your attitude in advance. Think directly and specifically about what you want to accomplish, in human terms, through the occasion that you're hosting—honoring a friend, celebrating someone's success, or giving your pals a good time. The details of what you do will serve your intention, but they aren't the heart of the matter. They don't deserve such a level of attention that you are drawn away from focusing on the people that motivated you to entertain in the first place.

If you find yourself becoming anxious, impatient, or irritated in the midst of an event, pause for a moment, and take a deep breath. Recall your earlier reflections on your reasons for having guests. Let your emotions settle down before you put yourself back into action. Then put a smile on your face and get on with the show.

This applies, as well, when your guests disappoint you. Sometimes, people don't rise to the good intentions and hopes that you have. Their lack of appreciation or thoughtfulness may feel hurtful, but it does not change the fact that you are doing something that counts. When you pause to breathe, remind yourself that their behavior is their problem, not yours. You are responsible only for yourself, and you've done your part.

Play host with a firm grasp of your intentions. Keep your guests front and center in your mind before and during your occasion. When you put first things first, the frazzle and fuss will have to take a backseat.

99.

Forgive Mistakes

We all make mistakes. Thus the saying, "To err is human." We let ourselves down sometimes when we entertain with a poorly planned event, a recipe gone awry, or a neglected invitation. Others let us down with their lateness, their failure to communicate, or thoughtlessness of one kind or another. Most of the time, the letdowns are not the result of malicious intent or character weakness, but rather of human error.

When mistakes happen—yours or someone else's—that have an unfortunate effect on your entertaining, it's time to put the second part of the saying above to work—"to forgive divine." The point of that phrase is not to suggest that only people make mistakes, while only God has the capacity and will to forgive. Instead, it is a reminder that when we err, we're simply doing what humans do. When we forgive, we are rising to a higher, better level.

Don't let mistakes get in the way of your relationships or enjoyment when you host an event. Take the sting out of errors by recognizing that everyone makes mistakes. It's virtually written into the definition of a human being. Don't stop there. Take the next step of forgiving. That means letting it go, no longer holding it against the person who erred, and moving on.

Did someone drop your grandmother's platter (with the chocolate soufflé that you labored over) on the floor? That could feel like a big, messy mistake as your guests sit restlessly at the table waiting for dessert. However, you gain nothing by making the platter or the dessert more important than the person who did the dropping, who is certainly feeling a great deal of embarrassment and pain. When you choose to forgive, you preserve your perspective and heal the wound.

Keep in mind that it is sometimes more difficult to forgive yourself than it is to forgive others. Don't make the mistake of holding yourself to a standard that no one can meet. Instead, treat yourself with the same loving care you extend to others. Cut others the same slack that you'd like them to cut you, and cut yourself the same slack that you would cut others. Life is too short to fuss over mistakes.

100.
Enjoy the Party

When all is said and done, your entertaining experience will be what it will be from one event to another. Sometimes, it will go just as planned, and you'll congratulate yourself on your skill. Other times, it will be full of surprises, and you'll wonder how it got that way.

No matter what you're planning or how it turns out, entertaining is a wonderful way of putting yourself in the mix of people who comprise your life. It gives you a chance to offer yourself and your resources in friendship and hospitality, and it allows you to punctuate everyday life with pleasure and creativity.

Instead of focusing on the outcome of your entertaining from one occasion to another, let it be to you what you want it to be to others— a joyful experience of community. Make it a point to be in the moment as you prepare for and welcome guests, thoroughly engaging in the camaraderie and exchange. Pay attention to the details of the time, taking in the full texture and flavor of the assembled guests, the conversation, the refreshments, and the activities.

Remember to keep your sense of humor activated. Even disasters have an element of the comic in them, and laughter is sound medicine in the face of stress. Look for the light side in the good experiences, as well as the bad. A twinkle in your eye shared with your guests can go a long way toward redeeming a less-than-ideal gathering.

Most of all, remember to be grateful for the company that you keep. Be glad for the good health to play host and the wherewithal to be generous. Be conscious of the people that you invite and all that makes them special. Give yourself to the enjoyment of the moment. Today will never come again. It is a gift.